İstanbul - 2012 / 1433

Published by:

Erkam Publications

Ikitelli Organize Sanayi Bölgesi

Turgut Özal Cd. No: 117 Kat: 2/C
Başakşehir, Istanbul, Turkey

Tel: +90 212 671 07 00 pbx
Fax: +90 212 671 07 48
E-mail: info@islamicpublishing.net

Web site: http://islamicpublishing.net

ISBN   : 978-9944-83-195-6

The author   : Osman Nuri Topbaş
Translator   : Ali Köse, Rahim Acar
Copy Editor   : R.Terri Harris
Graphics   : Zakir Shadmanov (Worldgraphics)
Printed by   : Erkam Printhouse

Such a Mercy He Was

Moral Legacy of Propet Muhammad

Osman Nuri Topbaş

ERKAM PUBLICATIONS

CONTENTS

CONTENTS ⌇⌇

PREFACE

All praise is due to Allah the Almighty, most compassionate, most beneficent, who treats us with mercy and benevolence, forgiving our sins. And may peace be upon our master, Prophet Muhammad ﷺ, who was sent as a mercy to the worlds, and is the healer, harbinger, and intercessor of humanity.

All existence in the universe rests upon Allah's love and mercy, and Allah the Almighty treats humans with special benevolence. Even those without faith draw breath and find sustenance thanks to Allah's mercy. Though it witnesses many kinds of cruelty, corruption, and rebellion, still the world is sustained through the endless mercy of Allah.

It is clear that Allah loves mercy and compassion, for divine mercy encompasses divine wrath. Allah describes His last messenger, Prophet Muhammad, peace and blessings be upon him,[1] as a mercy for the worlds, saying:

And We have not sent you save as a mercy to the worlds. (Anbiya', 12/107).

---

1. *Salla Allahu `alayhi wa sallam*, the benediction proper to the name of the Prophet, shall be indicated hereafter by ﷺ. The same sign shall be used for `alayhi as-salam*, "peace be upon him," the benediction proper to all prophets.

Everything that exists avails itself of this mercy, but it is humans who derive the greatest advantage. All the benefactions we are granted are nothing but divine bounties shining from that Sun of Mercy. All the beauties and harmonies of Nature are expressions of it. It is such a mercy that the colorful wings of a butterfly, the elegance of a blossoming rose, the daintiness of spring flowers, the virtues of humans, and the divine qualities that have nurtured many noble personalities are all reflections and favors of its beneficence. And human beings reach felicity and salvation only by following the higher norms of morality exemplified by the Greatest of Characters, Prophet Muhammad ﷺ, who is a unique guide for humanity.

Thus, all existence is always indebted to him. We ourselves can pay this debt by sending benedictions to him and loving him very much. To love him requires loving those whom he loves as well, so love for members of his family should also find room in our hearts. Among them are the great rightly-guided caliphs: Hadrat Abu Bakr, may Allah be pleased with him,[2] who was given the title of "the most faithful"; Hadrat ʿUmar ﷺ, who became the model for justice; Hadrat ʿUthman ﷺ, who was a monument of conscience and honesty; and Hadrat Ali ﷺ, the Gate of Knowledge, whom the Prophet ﷺ loved dearly. We should enjoy and follow the spiritual principles we have inherited from them all.

Such principles of life can save humanity from atrocities and cruelty, and consequently from eternal punishment, and lead us to an age of wellbeing. Our ignorance of such divine principles is a disaster for morality and justice, righteousness and knowledge. Society and its government, however, can only stand on the cornerstones of knowledge, morality, and justice. We can take respon-

---

2. *Radiya Allahu ʿanhu,* or *ʿanha,* the benediction proper to names of the Companions of the Prophet, shall be indicated hereafter by ﷺ.

sibility for this reality only through a voluntary adoption of the appropriate values.

We must reflect deeply in order to espouse those values rightly. Such reflection can only be undertaken in a spiritual atmosphere, not in an atmosphere flooded with selfish desires. Thus it is essential to educate both the intellect and the heart in the light of the divine messages. One may reach a degree of light either through the company of the righteous or through following the spiritual guidance of our learned masters. Among them is our chief master, Hadrat Mawlana Jalaluddin Rumi, may Allah sanctify his secret,[3] who has the greatest of talents for bringing hearts to maturity.

A life adorned with spiritual blessings is meant to be lived with mercy and compassion. Such blessings emanate from the Prophet Muhammad ﷺ, who is *a mercy to the worlds*. That Prophet of Mercy has given us, as a gift, principles for living every moment of our lives. One such principle important at the present time is to free ourselves from the habit of waste.

Today one may easily observe waste of faith and practice, waste of time, waste of learning, waste of moral sensitivity, waste of spiritual reflection, waste of livelihood and philanthropy, and waste of health and sustenance, not to mention waste of human beings themselves.

Muslims should deplore all this. We should endeavor to educate our children, who are entrusted to us by Allah, to live life in the spiritual atmosphere of the Qur'an and in the tradition of the Prophet, as a faithful generation. Muslims must maintain the delicate line between what is permitted and what is forbidden in all circumstances, putting aside empty excuses.

---

3. *Qaddasa Allahu sirrahu or sirraha*, the benediction proper to the names of spiritual heroes, shall hereafter be indicated by ﷺ.

Love for capital and other worldly possessions rules us, whereas we ought to be ruling worldly possessions. Charity, compassion, and altruism should be the hallmark of Muslims. We need to breathe, act, and speak with mercy at all times, just as the Prophet did. If we are to merit Paradise, then, we must revise our lives. We badly need the light of those principles shown forth in the life of the Prophet of Mercy. We need some shaking up if we are to find our true selves!

This book aims to help readers discover how our lives might be oriented toward living truly well. Earlier versions of some chapters have been published in the monthly journal *Altınoluk*.

May our Lord accept our prayers and reward our good will, and show us mercy.

O Lord! Please help us achieve the manner of the Prophet who has always been *tender toward the faithful*. (Tawbah, 9/128). Please grant us your mercy!

Amin....

Introduction

We need to internalize the moral character of the Prophet ﷺ so that we can pay our debt of gratitude to him and protect our faith in a spiritual atmosphere. Adherence to Allah comes first; then comes adherence and loyalty to the Prophet ﷺ, the eternal honor of the universe, since his affection and mercy for his community are stronger than a mother's for her child.

INTRODUCTION

Our Lord did not send the Prophet 🕌 *save as a mercy to the worlds*. Such a mercy he was that all creation came into being due to his existence, and all beings are ranked by Allah in proportion to their love for him.

• Such a mercy he was that his compassion and beneficence surround all humanity, even all creation.

• Such a mercy he was that he was granted to all souls and minds as a fountain of life, love, and wisdom; knowledge and learning; adorned with endless blessing.

• Such a mercy he was that the Qur'an, a guide to the true path, was endowed through him.

• Such a mercy he was that he became unique among Messengers. As the dearest to Allah, he was granted the spiritual Night Journey through the heavens and into the presence of Allah.

• Such a mercy he was that without him, all worlds would turn into a desolate desert.

• Such a mercy he was that the origin of creation emerged with his glorious being. All previous Messengers were aware of his glorious and blessed being.

• Such a mercy he was that all beauties are reflections of him. No flower blossoms without a hint of his light. No bloom would unfold without him. He is a spiritual rosebud, made up of glorious substance, which does not fade, but freshens day by day.

• Such a mercy he was that Allah Almighty Himself proclaims his merit and value by praising him.

Allah's compliment to him is above all other tributes. Allah proclaims that He Himself, along with His angels, blesses the Prophet – the beauty, the eternal pride of the universe – before decreeing that all the faithful should call for blessings upon him and salute him with a salutation. (Ahzab, 33/56).

What a grace for us, to have been granted the honor of the Chosen Prophet among the 124,000 prophets sent by Allah! Such a blessing from Allah is an exceptional one. It therefore behooves us to be thankful and express gratitude. To be a follower of the Sultan of the Prophets bestows honor, but also places a huge responsibility upon a Muslim's shoulders, for Allah Almighty has declared that obedience or disobedience shown toward the Prophet ﷺ is at one with obedience or disobedience shown toward Allah Himself.

Muslims are meant to manifest gratitude by holding the Prophet ﷺ closer than everything in this world and by loving him more than we love ourselves. We are supposed to praise the Prophet by calling down Allah's benedictions upon him whenever his name is mentioned; by spiritually benefiting from his life example; and by loving him. We should esteem him as the model and the reference for establishing our ideal Muslim personality and lifestyle. We depend upon his universal compassion in this world, and his intercession for our salvation in the Hereafter.

We are obliged to establish a way of life that allows us to be in union with him in all our acts and words, because *each person will be together what he* (or she) *loves,* and should therefore take his or her beloved as an example. The more we commit ourselves to the tradition of the Prophet, the more we experience love for him and feel him closer to our souls. The more we know and remember him, the more we orient ourselves to him. Thus we are intended to observe closely his perfect manners and personality, to follow him by adopting his perfect morality, and to feel him deep down in our hearts.

Our Messenger was not nurtured by humans, but by Allah. He was nurtured so well that he manifested the highest potentials of human personality. He was sent to all humanity as the interpreter of the invisible and unknown world, and as the teacher of the school of the Lord. No book can exhaust his boundless beauties, yet let us recount some examples.

Prophet Muhammad ﷺ: deeply concerned for his community

The compassion that the Prophet ﷺ felt for his community was even greater than that which a mother feels for her child. It is said in the Qur'an:

Certainly an Apostle has come to you from among yourselves; grievous to him is your falling into distress, deeply concerned is he for you; to the believers (he is) compassionate. (Tawbah, 9/128).

The Prophet ﷺ said countless prayers of mercy and compassion for his community. One day the Prophet ﷺ wept while praying, "O Allah! Please save my community, show Your mercy to them!." Allah Almighty asked the angel Gabriel to find out why the

Messenger had wept. When Gabriel asked the Prophet ﷺ about his tears, he said he had wept out of concern for his community. When Gabriel returned with this report, Allah Almighty said, "O Gabriel! Convey this good news to Muhammad: 'We will make you happy, not sorry, about your people." (Muslim, Iman 346).

✿

Ibn Mas`ud narrates a story that shows the level of the compassion the Prophet ﷺ showed toward his community.

Once, the Prophet ﷺ said: "O Ibn Mas`ud! Please recite a few verses of the Qur'an for us!" And I answered: "O Messenger of Allah! The Qur'an was revealed to you. It is not for me to recite it to you!" The Messenger said, "I too like listening to the Qur'an from someone else." Then I started to recite Surah Nisa' from the Qur'an. While I was reciting the verse, *"How will it be, then, when We bring from every people a witness and bring you as a witness against these?"* (Nisa', 4/41), the Prophet ﷺ said, "You had better stop reciting!" I looked at the Prophet and saw tears flowing from his eyes. (Bukhari, Tafsir 4/9; Muslim, Musafirin 247).

This story demonstrates the Prophet's concern for his community. On the Day of Judgment, it will be said

Read your book; your own self is sufficient as a reckoner against you this day (Isra' 17/14)

and the sins of the people will be disclosed. The Prophet ﷺ, who had a compassionate heart for his community, shed tears, for the above verse reminded him of what we will be facing in the Hereafter.

✿

The Prophet ﷺ once said, "Allah Almighty gave me two promises. The first is, *Allah will not punish them while you are among them.* The second is, *Allah will not punish them while yet they ask for forgiveness* (Anfal, 8/33). When I go, I will leave with my community the second promise, which will save them from the punishment of Allah until the Day of Judgment." (Tirmidhi, Tafsir 8/3082).

We may well hope that Allah Almighty will save from Hell His servants who love the Prophet ﷺ with all their hearts. We may well hope He will not permit such hearts to be burnt by fire.

These narratives are only a few of the many examples of the Prophet's endless compassion toward his community. We should always monitor our inner world in order to see how successful we are in following his tradition and responding to his compassion.

Prophet Muhammad ﷺ: the modest one

To Muhammad ﷺ, Prophethood did not mean temporal glory. Though there have been prophets who were kings, he preferred to be a servant of Allah rather than a king.[4] He busied himself with the problems of his community. He offered assistance to the needy. He assigned living space at one corner of the mosque to the poor among his Companions, and he personally looked after those Companions, who worked hard to learn the religion of Islam.

His humility was extraordinary. He never concerned himself with his own interests. His sole concern was to help people find the true path so that they could reach salvation both in this world and the Hereafter.

---

4.   Haythami, *al-Majmu`a az-Zawa'id*, IX: 192.

Hadrat A'ishah 🌸 talked about how the Prophet 🌸 used to help her with the housework. "My father Abu Bakr sent us a leg of mutton one night. The Prophet 🌸 held it while I tried to cut it up, and I held it while he tried to cut it up." One of the listeners asked A'ishah whether they had attempted this in the dark. Hadrat A'ishah answered, "When we had oil to put in the oil lamp, we preferred to use that oil for food. The family of the Prophet used to spend months without a piece of bread, or without boiling a kettle for food at home." (Ahmad, VI:217; Ibn Sa'ad, I:405).

Prophet Muhammad 🌸: the generous one

One day, someone asked the Prophet 🌸 to give him something to eat. The Prophet 🌸 said: "I have nothing I can give you, but you can buy something in my name, and I will pay for it later when I have some money." Hadrat 'Umar 🌸 overheard the conversation. He did not like seeing the Prophet 🌸 in difficulty. He said: "O Messenger! If you have, you can give, but if you do not have, you are not supposed to give. Before Allah, you are not responsible to give what you do not have!"

The Prophet 🌸 was not happy with what Hadrat Umar said. Seeing this, another companion said, "O Messenger, may my mother and father be sacrificed for you! You ought to give. Do not fear that the Lord of the Universe will cut your rations!" The Prophet 🌸 smiled at these words, for they mirrored his wishes. He replied, "I am ordained to do so anyway." (Haythami, X, 242).

❋

When a poor person came to the door of the Prophet 🌸, he used first to ask his household what there was home. If he learned that they had nothing but water, he would then ask his Companions to meet that person's needs. And he would not be satisfied until he knew that those needs had been met. Another example of this kind is told by Anas ﷺ.

"Some goods were brought to the Prophet from Bahrain. The Prophet ﷺ said: "Let all goods be placed in the mosque." The Messenger of Allah had never previously received a greater amount.. He went to perform the prayer. Afterwards he stood by the goods and gave them away to passersby until nothing was left for himself." (Bukhari, Salat 42).

The Prophet ﷺ used to find great joy in giving joy to the faithful by meeting their needs. Once he said: "Angel Gabriel conveyed the words of Allah Almighty when He said: *"This religion* [Islam] *is the one that I choose for you and with which I am content."* Only generosity and good morality go with religion. Make this religion exalted with these two characteristics as long as you live as Muslims." (Haythami, VIII, 20; Ali al-Muttaqi, *al-Kanz* VI: 392). Thus it is our duty to adhere to the moral principles that the Prophet ﷺ displayed so that we might elevate our religion and spiritually rescue our faith.

Our first loyalty must be to Allah, our second to the Prophet ﷺ. That is the due of one who prayed for his community before he prayed for himself, and who, when he made his own sacrifice, provided sacrificial animals for all those in his community who could not afford their own.[5] Our loyalty reaches it zenith when, moved by great love and fondness, we make his way of life a spiritual source for all our own conduct. The Prophet ﷺ described how dearly he loves the devout members of his community who follow his way: "Some of those who love me best will appear after my time. They will be willing to sacrifice their property and households for the chance of seeing me." (Muslim, Jannah 12).

---

5.   Abu Dawud, Adahi, 3-4; ibn Sa'd, I, 249.

If we cannot manage to follow the principles set by the Prophet ﷺ, we will experience losses and perhaps even waste our lives suffering painful contradictions between our inner and outer drives. This is so because Allah created the human being with two sets of characteristics: both those that draw us to Him, and those that alienate us from Him, attractive though these vices may be. It is said in the Qur'an:

"Then He inspired it [the human self] *to understand what is right and wrong for it. He will indeed be successful who purifies it."* (Surah Shams, 8-9).

The inner worlds of those who are not spiritually trained in the light of the Qur'an and the tradition of the Prophet are like forests holding many animals, from the wildest to the tamest. Each person, according to his or her nature, houses the character of an animal. Some are as sly as foxes, some are as ferocious as hyenas, some are as ambitious and greedy as ants, and some are as poisonous as snakes. Some will bite you if you stroke them, some will suck your blood, and some will smile in your face while stabbing you in the back. Each of these characteristics is embodied in a different animal.

People who cannot manage to save themselves from enslavement to their lower inclinations are unable to build a firm personality. Some of them house the characters of one or two animals, others house the characteristics of many animals. And since people's inner worlds pervade all their behavior, a wise person can easily notice what characters they are harboring inside.

Was not Communism, a system founded on the blood of 20 million people, the product of wild inner worlds? Are not the pyramids, built for the corpses of single pharaohs at the expense of uncounted workers who were buried alive, monuments to relentless tyranny? The past holds many lessons for those who are still ignorant, yet one can easily witness today examples of tyranny and torment that would surprise even the most savage hyena. They all reveal that if a society is dominated by frog-natured people, swamps will spread. If a society is dominated by snake-natured people, all will be poisoned: terror and anarchy will spread. And if a society is dominated by rose-natured and merciful people, rose gardens will spread: society will find real peace.

All this is visible from history. In history, it is the Prophet Muhammad ﷺ, master of all the prophets, who was the unique figure, for it was he who turned time and space into a garden. Over 23 years of mission, he offered humanity a rose garden that does not fade. During his time of prophethood, the right and the wrong, in their entirety, became crystal-clear. Human perceptions about the creator, the universe, and the nature of the self were all clarified by him. At that time, humans grasped that this world is a testing ground. An ignorant society turned into a society based on knowledge.[6] Believers began to understand that the human body emerges from a drop of water, that birds emerge from eggs, and that trees and vegetables emerge from seeds. The faithful began to contemplate the logic and meaning of creation, and their souls set out toward infinite horizons of wisdom.

It was the Prophet's training which permitted the community he led to develop the highest degree of compassion, devotion, sacrifice, and sensitivity toward justice.. The Messenger became the center of a fellowship whose life was founded upon winning the pleasure of Allah. All hearts were then filled with the excitement of the quest. Everyone asked, "What does Allah wants from us? In

---

6.   See as-Zumar, 39: 9.

what condition would the Prophet ﷺ wish to see us?" In this way, night turned into day, and winter turned into spring. Thus that age of human history became a true Golden Age.

So gracious was the Messenger of Allah that through his presence, many dark wells were filled with glorious light. All that lies behind the smear campaigns against him which surface from time to time is the ignorance of slanderers, and their evil intentions.

Every living being survives in the environment appropriate to its nature. This natural law holds for humans as well. Bees require blooming flowers, and cannot live without them. Rats inhabit filthy places, and do not flourish in rose gardens. In just this way, sublime souls are nurtured by the glory emanating from the Reality of Muhammad. Evil souls thrive in malice.

Hadrat Abu Bakr ﷺ used to look at the face of the Prophet ﷺ and say in amazement, "O my Lord! What a beautiful face!" What Abu Bakr was witnessing was own his inner world reflected in the Prophet's face. Thus when the Prophet ﷺ said: "I have not made use of anyone else's property as I have used the property of Abu Bakr," Abu Bakr replied in tears, "O Messenger of Allah! Do not I and my property belong you?" (Ibn Maja, Muqaddimah 11). These words are clear evidence that Abu Bakr committed himself so fully to the Prophet ﷺ that he united himself with him. He made his inner world a mirror for the Prophet. On the other hand, Abu Jahl, the chief enemy of Allah and His Messenger, used to have an aversion for the face of the Prophet. Looking at him, he would not receive a positive reflection, but was confronted by his own faithlessness and violence. Each saw his own real personality, his inner world, in the Prophet's face.

Prophets are like shining mirrors. In them, everyone sees his or her image, his or her inner world. No mirror lies to the person who gazes at it. Mirrors reflect the true image of the one who looks.

It is well-known that venomous tongues and senseless writings gravely offend innocent religious people who love the Prophet ﷺ dearly. Those who make themselves the enemies of the Muslims, the Qur'an, and the Prophet will, sooner or later, face the revenge of Allah Almighty. It is He who is the safeguard of the religion of Islam.

It should be noted well that it is impossible to erase humans' innate tendency toward what is right. Allah Almighty has endowed humans with this spiritual hunger. No matter how many efforts are undertaken to spread atheism, the beautiful flowers of religion, rooted in the spiritual depths of human beings, will emerge into life. The need of servants to come closer to their Lord can never be stopped. Such sublime feelings cannot be terminated, because it is divine power that has established them. The innate form of human beings is to come closer to Allah and to have need of a religion.

May Allah illuminate our hearts and eyes with the light of the Prophet ﷺ ! May Allah help us be among the community of the Sultan of the Prophets! May Allah bless our hearts with felicity from the climate of the golden age of the Prophet! May Allah make us sincere servants to Him, and deserving followers of the Prophet ﷺ !

Amin..

Examples from the life of the Prophet ﷺ

Norms For A Sublime Morality - 1

We should take the exemplary personality of the Messenger of Allah as a guide at every moment of our lives. Every benediction of Allah that we invoke upon the Prophet ﷺ is aimed at bringing us reflections from his spiritual life. Any Muslim who manages to adopt such noble characteristics of the Prophet ﷺ as humility, acceptance, and submission can easily reach real happiness and salvation.

CHAPTER 1

Examples from the life of the Prophet ﷺ
NORMS FOR A SUBLIME MORALITY – 1

A believer can develop a perfect spiritual character only by adopting the sublime morality of the Prophet ﷺ. This aim is achievable to the degree that one loves the Prophet, the pride of the universe, and reveres his example.

From the blessed tongue of the Messenger of Allah, humanity heard heavenly words that cured and illuminated hearts. Through the agency of the Messenger, the glory of creation, human beings are granted an endless ocean of forgiveness It is due to the Messenger, the master of the universe, that the human race is addressed by Allah the Almighty with the words *"O My servants!"*

In the face of all these blessings of Allah, we, as the people of Muhammad, ought live according to his way, doing wholeheartedly what he enjoined us to do and abstaining from what he forbade us.

Allah the Almighty granted the most honorable position, the "praised station," (*al-maqam al-mahmud*) to the Prophet ﷺ. Allah also counseled the Prophet as befit his honorable position. And since the Prophet ﷺ was so *tender and affectionate* toward his people, he invited us to join him, that we might follow together the path which Allah showed him. Here are some of those counsels.

The Prophet said 🌸, "My Lord bade me to fear Him at all times, whether alone or in public. I advise you to follow me in that."[7] In order to follow this guidance, he meticulously kept all the orders of Allah, commenting, ""I swear by Allah that I am the one among you who fears, submits to, and respects Allah the most!" (Sahih Bukhari, Nikah 1).

⊛

When he was about to leave a group of people, the Prophet always prayed "O Allah! Please give us a portion of that fear which will place a barrier between us and sins!" (Tirmidhi, Da`awat 79).

⊛

The Prophet 🌸 had the honor of knowing Allah more deeply than any other human being. He once said to the Companions: "If you were to know what I know, you would laugh less and cry more." Upon hearing these words the Companions burst into tears. (Bukhari, Tafsir 5/12).

⊛

Allah the Almighty promises Paradise to His servants who fear Him in secret or in public. It is said in the Qur'an:

And as for him who fears to stand in the presence of his Lord and forbids the soul from low desires, then surely the Garden - that is the abode. (Nazi`at, 79/40-41).

And

This is what you were promised: (it is) for everyone who turns frequently (to Allah]) and keeps (His limits), who fears the Beneficent Allah in secret and comes with a penitent heart. (Qaf, 50/32-33).

---

7. For this saying of the Prophet see İbrahim Canan, *Hadis Ansiklopedisi*, XVI, 252, no. 5838.

And

Their sides draw away from (their) beds; they call upon their Lord in fear and in hope, and they spend (benevolently) out of what We have given them. (Sajdah, 32/16).

The nights of the Messengers and Friends of Allah, which they spend in fear of Allah and in hope of His beneficence, are brighter than the day, for their nights are filled with the serenity and spirituality of their prostration in tears.

❀

The Prophet ﷺ said: "My Lord ordained me to judge with justice whether in times of anger or of peace. (I do advise the same to you)." One may easily leave a balanced position for an extreme one in times of anger, and judge unjustly. But we should remember Allah and the Hereafter and act in patience, not incline to injustice.

❀

Our Lord says in the Qur'an:

O you who believe! Be maintainers of justice, bearers of witness of Allah's sake, though it may be against your own selves..." (Nisa', 4/135).

And

... act equitably; surely Allah loves those who act equitably. (Hujurat, 49/9).

❀

Touching upon several issues, The Prophet ﷺ said, "There are three conditions of salvation: to act justly in times of anger as well as peace; to spend moderately not only in poverty but also in wealth; and to fear Allah both in private and public. (Haythami, I:90).

❀

A person of high rank came to the Prophet to ask him to sus-
pend the punishment of a thief . The Prophet ﷺ answered him: "I
would carry out that punishment even if the culprit were my daughter Fatimah." (Bukhari, Anbiya' 54; Muslim, Hudud 8, 9).[8]

✤

Justice is essential for the welfare of individuals and society
alike. Therefore Hadrat `Umar ﷺ said: "Justice is essential to a suc-
cessful government."

✤

During the reign of `Umar ibn `Abdul-`Aziz, who reigned
for only two and half years in the 92-year-long `Umayyad period
and is held to be the fifth great caliph of Islam, the people of the
`Umayyad state lived in peace and security because of equitable and
just governance. Cruelty does not bring peace, and states cannot
stand without justice. The story of a Christian architect who sued
the Ottoman sultan, Mehmed the Second, is an historic example in
this regard. Though the judge of the court, Hizir Bey, was a close
friend of the Sultan, his verdict was nonetheless against the Sultan.
This story shows how the Ottomans regarded justice to be fundamental to state governance.

✤

The Prophet ﷺ said: "My Lord ordained me to spend moderately in poverty and in wealth. (I do advise the same to you)."
Whether Allah has decreed us to be poor or rich, we should spend
moderately, and never waste. The Prophet ﷺ advised us to appreciate wealth before we face poverty.[9]

Allah the Almighty delineates how to spend moderately:

---

8. Bukhari, al-Maghazi 53; Nasa`i, al-Qat` al-Sariq, 6, VIII, 72-74.
9. Hakim, *al-Mustadrak*, IV:341.

...and do not squander wastefully. Surely the squanderers are the fellows of the devils, and Satan is ever ungrateful to his Lord. (Isra', 17/26-27).

And do not keep your hand shackled to your neck nor stretch it forth to the utmost (limit) of its stretching forth, lest you should (afterwards) sit down blamed, destitute. (Isra', 17/29).

❉

The Prophet ﷺ said: "Those who spend moderately and keep away from wastefulness will never grow poor." (Ibn Hanbal, I:477). And, "Whoever asks Allah to decide between two or more courses of action by consultative prayer (*istikharah*)[10]* will not be disappointed; and whoever asks advice will not regret; and whoever spends moderately will not grow poor." (Haythami, *al-Majmu`ah al-zawa'id*, II:280). A believer should be aware that sovereignty belongs to Allah, and that the human being, as a deputy of Allah, holds worldly possessions only temporarily. We should spend only as much as we need upon ourselves, and spend the rest in the way of Allah.

Allah says in the Qur'an:

...And they ask you as to what they should spend. Say: What you can spare. (Baqarah, 2/219).

❉

The Prophet ﷺ advised us to be rich in heart even when we are not rich materially: "Save yourself from the Fire by giving charity, even half a date. And let those of you who cannot find even that much save yourselves from the Fire by saying good words." (Bukhari, Adab 34).

❉

10.   * To seek divine help through prayer and dreams.

Real welfare comes through spending in the way of Allah. One can serve and spend in the way of Allah only by earning through legitimate means, not yearning for material benefits. The Prophet ﷺ said in this regard, "Legitimate and useful goods, in the hands of a righteous person, are beyond praise." (Ibn Hanbal, IV:202).

❋

Righteous believers are compassionate and affectionate. Compassion requires us to give what we have to those who do not have it. Indeed, compassion requires that we rush to meet the needs of the deprived. Compassion and generosity bring a Muslim both spiritual tranquility in this world and salvation in the Hereafter.

❋

Those who are rich and thankful, and those who are poor and patient, are both rare. Both groups are valuable servants in the eyes of Allah. People who are rich but generous and thankful, and people who are poor but honorable and patient, are equal in human esteem, and both win the pleasure of Allah. However, people who are rich but arrogant and miserly; and people who are poor but rebellious and impatient, are both dispraised in Islam. The Prophet ﷺ said, "O Lord! I seek refuge in you from the evil testing of wealth and poverty." (Muslim, Dhikr 49). Thus, those who have the spiritual characters of contentment, acceptance, and submission are the truly wealthy. And one can maintain the joy of such wealth only by spending in the way of Allah.

❋

When a campaign was begun to raise resources for the Battle of Tabuk in the way of Allah, the poor Companions did their best to join that campaign by making sacrifices either from their efforts or from their limited possessions. One of these was Abu `Aqil ﷺ who earned two pails of dates by working all night. He brought one pail to his household and gave away the second for the Battle of Tabuk. The Prophet 🕮 said to him, "May Allah multiply both the pail you left at home and the one you brought here!" (Tabari, Tafsir, X:251).

❁

The Prophet 🕮 said, "Once one dirham of charity was rewarded more than a hundred thousand dirhams!" The Companions asked: "How did that happen?" The Prophet 🕮 replied, "One man had only two dirhams of goods. He took half of it – namely, one dirham – and gave it away. Another man, a very rich one, took one hundred thousand dirhams of his merchandise and gave it to charity." (Nasa`i, Zakat 49). The first man gave away half of what he had. The second contributed far more than the first, but his gift was only a fraction of his assets. Thus the value of our alms comes not from how much we give away, but from how sensitive we are in terms of self-sacrifice. The following story also points out this fact.

A man came into the presence of Hadrat `Uthman 🕮 saying, "O wealthy people! I admire you. You get all the blessings by giving charity, emancipating slaves, and going on the Pilgrimage!"

Hadrat `Uthman asked him: "Do you really admire us?"

The man said: "Yes, I do really admire you!"

Hadrat `Uthman replied: "I swear by Allah that just one dirham of charity given by a poor man under difficult conditions is more valuable than ten thousand dirhams contributed by a rich one." (Ali al-Muttaqi, VI, 612/17098).

Shaykh Sa`di gives the following advices in this regard: "Allah the Almighty does not close the door of goodness to anyone. So know that everyone's goodness is measured according to his or her capacity. A poor man's small amount of alms is more valuable than a rich man's huge amount. The leg of a locust is a huge burden for an ant."

Thus the value of almsgiving or doing favors is evaluated according to the level of the sacrifice involved. The story of the three martyrs of Islam in the Battle of Yarmuk, when they all offered the only cup of water they had to one another before their last gasp, is a good example in this regard.

❁

The ideal of the Companions was to identify with the moral character of the Prophet ﷺ. In this way they managed to reach the zenith of compassion and ascetic life *(zuhd)*. They lived in complete devotion, following the life principles of the Prophet ﷺ. They refrained from all forms of extravagance and waste. The rich among them were thankful, and the poor were patient. The selfless attitude of the Prophet ﷺ in the distribution of war booty is an example of how he was thankful in times of abundance, and his binding a stone over his belly so as not to feel the pains of hunger is an example how he was patient in times of poverty.

❁

The Prophet ﷺ said, "Allah the Almighty ordained me to visit my kin even though they do not keep in touch with me. (I advise the same to you)." Allah the Almighty urges His servants to maintain relationships with family and to treat them kindly. Emphasizing the importance of visiting and looking after kin, the Prophet ﷺ said, "Allah sent me with a mission to maintain kinship, to destroy idols,. and to affirm the Oneness of Allah, not attributing partners to Him." (Muslim, Musafirin 294).

It is incumbent on us, due to our faith, to keep in touch with family and to let them know, gently, what we are all invited to by

Allah, even though they may not respond to our concern for them. The Prophet ﷺ said, "Returning favors to your kin does not mean that your responsibility toward them is fulfilled. The one who fulfills that responsibility keeps on doing favors despite their not being returned, and stays in touch with those who do not stay in touch themselves." (Bukhari, Adab 15; Abu Dawud, Zakah 45).

❈

The Prophet ﷺ is again the best example in this regard. Whenever he slaughtered an animal he sent some part of it to the relatives of his wife Khadijah ﷺ (Bukhari, al-Manaqib al-Ansar 20).

❈

The Prophet ﷺ again said: "Learn your family tree so that you can keep your relationship with its members." (Ali al-Muttaqi, *al-Kanz*, X:220, no. 29162).

❈

Allah the Almighty says in the Qur'an that those who ignore visiting kin and do not look after them will be losers:

...those who break the covenant of Allah after its confirmation and cut asunder what Allah has ordered to be joined (faith and kinship ties), and make mischief in the land; these it is who are the losers."(Baqarah, 1/27).

[O hypocrites!] *But if you held command, you would be sure to make mischief in the land and to cut off the ties of kinship! These it is whom Allah has cursed; He has made them deaf and blind.*" (Muhammad, 47/22-23).

The Prophet ﷺ also said that those who ignore visiting kin will be in grave loss. He said, "Those who cut off the ties of kinship cannot deserve Paradise." (Bukhari, Adab 11) And he said, "Allah the Almighty will punish two groups of people in the Hereafter: tyrants, and those who neglect their kin. These two groups are also those who deserve most to be punished in worldly life." (Abu Dawud, Adab 43; Tirmidhi, Qiyamah 57).

❀

The Prophet ﷺ said, "My Lord ordered me to give to the one who took from me. (I do advise the same to you)." It is said in the Qur'an:

"And not alike are the good and the evil. Repel (evil) with what is best, when lo! he between whom and you was enmity would be as if he were a warm friend." (Fussilat, 41/34).

The Prophet ﷺ said, "Do not break off relations with whoever breaks relations with you! Give to whoever never gave to you! Forgive whoever harmed you!" (Ibn Hanbal, IV:148, 158).

❀

The people of Mecca suffered from famine and drought in the second year of the Hijrah. The Prophet ﷺ helped them, although they had fought against him for twenty years, by sending them gold, barley, and dates. It was Abu Sufyan who received these resources to distribute to the poor of the Quraysh.

A human being is bound to appreciate favors and good treatment. Such characteristics appease even an enemy. Even Abu Sufyan, the chief enemy of the Prophet, felt kindlier towards him because of his favor to the poor of Mecca. He said, "May Allah reward the son of my brother [the Prophet was Abu Sufyan's nephew]! He fulfilled the rights of his kin." (Yaqubi, *al-Tarikh*, II:56).

❀

Many people embraced Islam due to the Prophet's noble-hearted character.

⊛

The story of Prophet Joseph ﷺ is of another example in this regard. His brothers threw him into a well because they envied him. Yet Prophet Joseph treated them well many years after the event when he met them in the palace of the Sultan of Egypt as a vizier. Upon his favor to them, they said:

… By Allah! Now has Allah certainly chosen you over us, and we were certainly sinners. (Yusuf, 12/91).

⊛

It is incumbent upon us to find a way to the hearts of those we wish to direct to the true and virtuous path. The easiest way to do that is to exercise generosity, compassion, and forgiveness.

In order to be perfect believers and win the love of Allah, we should

- always bear in our hearts the fear of Allah;

- observe justice at all times, whether in anger or ease;

- spend in the way of Allah, spending moderately upon ourselves whether in wealth and poverty;

- keep in touch with kin;

- show honor even toward those who behave relentlessly toward us; and forgive even those who tyrannize us.

May Allah guide us to follow the counsel of the Prophet ﷺ as a shadow follows the one who casts it! May Allah adorn us with the moral character of the Prophet, who is the prime example for humanity, and include us among His righteous servants!

Amin…

CHAPTER 2

Examples from the Life of the Prophet

Norms For A Sublime Morality - 2

We should bear in mind that Allah the Almighty created humans to need one another. Any society contains both the rich and powerful and the poor and weak. One might well ask, "Why has Allah the Almighty permitted people to be poor?" And the answer is simple: Allah has entrusted the poor to the rich..

NORMS FOR A SUBLIME MORALITY – 2
Examples from the Life of the Prophet

Love attaches to everything related to the beloved. The Mountain of Uhud, for example, is not an ordinary mountain in the minds of Muslims, because the Prophet loved it. The city of Medina was an ordinary city, but it became a blessed one after the Hijrah, when the Prophet went to live there. That Illuminated City became dear to all Muslims because it was identified with the Prophet.

Thus love of Allah requires love of what Allah loves best, which is the Prophet. Allah the Almighty says in the Qur'an:

Say: If you love Allah, then follow me, Allah will love you... (Âl-i 'Imran, 3/31).

Therefore whoever endeavors to follow Allah and His Messenger will certainly be counted among the beloved servants, by the grace of Allah. Commitment to the way of Allah and His Messenger will necessarily lead the faithful into such spiritual traits as expressing love and mercy toward all creation for the sake of the Creator, sharing resources with the rest of the faithful, developing an ability to forgive others, and seeing creation through the eye of the Creator.

Like moths circling a flame, the Companions regarded spiritual union with the Prophet ﷺ as the greatest blessing in this world: therefore they received divine grace. And those Muslims who, throughout history, reflected in their persons the venerable character of the Prophet ﷺ matured the divine qualities inherent in their creation, and became pioneering torches of faith and morality for humanity.

The most effective medicine for the sick soul is to love and follow the Prophet ﷺ by admiring his extraordinary character.

Since the Prophet ﷺ desires to unite with his community in Paradise, he wants us to observe the rules of Allah. Allah the Almighty says in the Qur'an:

Certainly a Messenger has come to you from among yourselves; grievous to him is your falling into distress, excessively solicitous respecting you; to the believers (he is) compassionate. (Tawbah, 9/128).

We are, therefore, bound to take heed of what the Prophet ﷺ counseled us to follow so that we might unite with him by the pool of Kawthar, the most honorable part of Paradise. Here are some of those counsels.

The Prophet ﷺ said: "My Lord ordained me to reflect even when I am in silence. (I advise the same to you)."[11]

Allah the Almighty endowed all creatures with an ability to think in accordance with their capacities. In all living creatures except for humans and jinn, this ability takes the form of natural instincts for bodily survival. Instinct helps animals feed themselves, defend themselves, and breed.

Human beings, on the other hand, are endowed with the ability to reflect. This ability helps us to come closer to Allah and become

11. İbrahim Canan, *Hadis Ansiklopedisi,* XVI, 252, no. 5838.

His honorable servants. People are not supposed to use this special capacity merely for the pursuit of sensual pleasures in the world. That is indeed a grave mistake for humanity!

The more one reflects upon the wonders of creation and develops sensitivity in reflection, the greater one's taste of divine love and the peace of the Hereafter.

Reflection is the greatest tool for the attainment of our full human spiritual capacity The Qur'an, the ultimate guide to salvation, from first to last urges us to reflect deeply upon the wisdom in human creation, in the design of the universe, and in its own miraculous words. The Qur'an phrases its warnings in terms such as *"Do you not think?" "Do you not contemplate?" "Do you not understand the examples set out for humanity by the Qur'an?"* So anyone who wants to live a life attuned to human dignity should enter the atmosphere of reflection guided by the Qur'an.

Allah the Almighty says in the Qur'an:

Do they not reflect within themselves: Allah did not create the heavens and the earth and what is between the two but with truth, and (for) an appointed term? (Rum, 30/8).

Were We then fatigued with the first creation? Yet are they in doubt with regard to a new creation. And certainly We created man, and We know what his mind suggests to him, and We are nearer to him than his jugular vein. (Qaf, 50/15-16).

The Messenger of Allah reflected continually on Allah, the Creator of the Universe. He used to contemplate, without moving, for long periods. He invited his community also to reflect upon the creation,[12] and declared that contemplation is a uniquely valuable form of worship.[13]

⊛

The Prophet ﷺ said: "My Lord ordained for me that my speech should be remembrance of Allah. (I advise the same to you)."

Lovers have a desire to remember and to mention those they love. The more one remembers the beloved, the more love increases. Thus those who have once tasted faith in Allah will seek to increase their love through remembering Allah.

Remembering Allah does not necessarily mean reciting His holy names. It means intentionally internalizing the love of Allah in our hearts, at the center of our consciousness. It is therefore said in the Qur'an:

... now surely by Allah's remembrance are the hearts set at rest. (13/Ra`d, 28).

Hadrat A'ishah ﷺ narrated that the Prophet ﷺ was *always* in remembrance of Allah.[14] Allah the Almighty wants us to follow the Prophet ﷺ in that.

... and remember your Lord much and glorify Him in the evening and the morning. (Al `Imran, 3/41).

Then when you have finished the prayer, remember Allah standing and sitting and reclining. (Nisa', 4/103).

Allah the Almighty ordains in this verse that His servants should unite their hearts with Him at all times, and not give up on

---

12. Daylami, II, 56.
13. Ali al-Muttaqi, *al-Kanz al-Ummal*, XVI, 121.
14. Muslim, Hayd 117.

remembering Allah even in the midst of war, during times of fear and danger.

Remembrance of Allah is necessary to keep the heart on the straight path. The Qur'an says:

And be not like those who forsook Allah, so He made them forsake their own souls: these it is who are the transgressors. (Hashr, 59/19).

Allah the Almighty revealed to Moses and Aaron (peace be upon them) when they went to Pharaoh:

Go you and your brother with My communications and be not remiss in remembering Me. (Ta Ha, 20/42).

A believer whose heart remembers Allah with the words "O my Lord!" cannot speak anything but truth, cannot act with anything but justice, and shows mercy to all creation, because such attributes of Allah as the All-Compassionate and Most Merciful will manifest in the faithful who remember Allah and chant His names.

Whoever remembers Allah and unites his or her heart with Allah reaches the zenith of worship. The Prophet ﷺ says, "The difference between the person who remembers Allah and the person who does not is like the difference between the living and the dead." (Bukhari, Da`awat 66).

❀

Again the Prophet ﷺ said: "My Lord ordained for me to take lessons when I look at creation. (I advise the same to you)."

Allah the Almighty praises those servants who look at creation with the eye of insight and declares that He makes His verses (signs) understandable to such servants. The verses of the Qur'an urge humanity to take all happenings as lessons:

Will they not then consider the camels, how they are created? And the heaven, how it is reared aloft? And the mountains, how they are firmly fixed? And the earth, how it is made a vast expanse? (Ghashiyah, 88/17-20).

Have they not then journeyed in the land and seen what was the end of those before them: Allah brought down destruction upon them, and the unfaithful shall have the like of it. (Muhammad, /4710).

The most exalted form of knowledge, in science and spirituality alike, is to have a comprehensive understanding of the reality of being. Mawlana Jalaluddin Rumi ﷺ indicated his reaching this stage with such words as "I am roasted and burnt." In his *Mathnawi* he converses with all manner of creatures and reflects upon their feelings, interpreting their condition. One of these spiritual conversations is with the rose.

The rose received its fragrance through keeping company with the thorn. Listen to the rose to learn this! Hear what it says: Why should I worry myself when I am with the thorn? I learned to laugh through putting up with the ill-natured thorn. Through union with the thorn I achieved my ability to offer perfume to the universe.

Yunus Emre, a Turkish Sufi, conversed with a sunflower. He uttered the wisdom and secrets of the universe through the tongue of the sunflower.

Sa`di al-Shirazi said, "To intelligent minds, every leaf of every tree presents a book of the knowledge of Allah. To ignorant minds, all trees together do not offer a single leaf."

❁

Such spiritual qualities as reflection, remembrance of Allah, and taking lessons from creation are prerequisites to spiritual perfection through clarification of the inner world. The Prophet ﷺ acknowledged that Allah ordained him to cultivate such qualities strongly and advised his community to be careful in these matters.

Imam Rabbani put it eloquently: "What a good believer is the one blessed by following the example of the Prophet! Even tiny efforts performed with unshakable faith are deemed to be great efforts in these difficult days of Islam…" (*al-Maktubat al-Rabbani, letter 44*)

May Allah include us all among His fortunate servants who rightly follow the example of the Prophet. A lifestyle that follows the way of the Prophet ﷺ leads one to salvation in both this world and the next. The only prescription for happiness is found in the noble rules and merciful manner of the Prophet. That prescription turns worldly sufferings into eternal salvation, painful tears into everlasting smiles.

The religious observances we enjoy in this world should be attuned to these noble truths, for then we might be granted the eternal celebration. These principles include reflection, remembrance, and observation of creation. They also include adorning our lives with the morality of the Prophet ﷺ through altruism and sharing with other people.

We should bear in mind that Allah the Almighty created humans to need one another. Any society contains both the rich and powerful and the poor and weak. One might well ask, "Why has Allah the Almighty permitted people to be poor?" And the answer is simple: Allah has entrusted the poor to the rich. This responsibility to care is assigned by Allah Himself.

If the rich and powerful reflected that they could easily find themselves in the position of the weak and poor, they would take care of those in difficulty and fulfill their responsibilities by extending helping hands to the needy. For worldly life is transitory

– it is almost nothing compared to the eternal life of the Hereafter. Meanwhile, the needy may perhaps reach salvation in the Hereafter merely through of their patience and gratitude toward Allah in this world.

The Prophet ﷺ said: "I swear by Allah, in whose hand is my life, that you cannot enter Paradise unless you show mercy to one another." The Companions said, "O Messenger of Allah! We are all merciful to each other." The Prophet ﷺ answered: "I do not mean showing mercy to yourselves alone. I mean being merciful toward all creation – a mercy that includes the whole creation!" (Hakim, IV,185/7310).

Therefore we must take heed of the silent outcries within our society. Our major concerns must be the sick and old who live in desolation, orphans, youth enmeshed in alcohol and drugs, and those who suffer from ethnic or religious alienation.

When we extend our hands and hearts to the destitute and needy, it is our festival of joy. Muslims are the organs of a single body, so every single person who is alienated from us is like an organ disconnected from our body. Urging Muslims to maintain such an inclusive attitude, the Prophet ﷺ said, "Muslims are like a single body in loving one another, in expressing mercy to one another, and in defending one another. When one part of the body is sick, other parts of the body suffer restlessness and fever." (Bukhari, Adab 27; Muslim, Birr 66).

What can we do to reach the real festival of religion, when humanity finds salvation with the smiling face of Islam, the ignorant awaken, and the underprivileged rejoice? We should think hard about that. We need to spend time thinking about the religious festival of oppressed and aggrieved Muslims throughout the world. What sort of greeting card should we send them? How can we extend our hearts and prayers to fellow Muslims under oppression, to orphans, to the poor who feel like birds with broken wings? Might we make them smile for once? That might give us the pleasure of observing a real celebration.

The real festivals that lead to the real salvation will only be celebrated when we can give positive answers to such questions. How happy are those who live in accordance with the ethics of the Prophet!

May Allah help us feel deeply the sufferings of oppressed fellow Muslims throughout the world, make our hearts a warm ground for them, and reach them both through physical help and prayer. May Allah make the doors to the Hereafter an eternal festival adorned with spiritual happiness!

Amin…

Examples from the life of the Prophet

Norms For A Sublime Morality - 3

To transmit this religion well one needs a humble heart adorned with the wisdom of the Qur'an and a pleasant face reflecting the smiling nature of Islam. One should be a symbol of what is good and right and speak the language of the heart.

Examples from the life of the Prophet ﷺ

NORMS FOR A SUBLIME MORALITY – 3

Allah the Almighty created all beings, and human beings in particular, with an inclination to love. The spiritual progress humans make depends on the degree to which we can direct our love toward Allah and toward the doing of good deeds in this world, which is a divine classroom where we are examined by Allah. The unique and final goal of life is a love through which our souls can find peaceful settlement is Allah the Almighty, who breathed from His soul into ours. Every kind of ephemeral love that is directed to a mistaken object wanders in blind alleys. If our love does not reach Allah, it ends in nothing but exhaustion for the soul.

Mawlana Jalaluddin Rumi remarked on our ignorance in this regard, "It is not surprising to see a lamb running from a wolf, since the wolf is an enemy and a predator of lambs. What is surprising is to see a lamb falling in love with a wolf!"

Our nature and welfare require us to make the love of Allah the center of our lives. Therefore all other transitory loves should build a ladder for us toward divine love. This is a primordial goal of the creation of humanity.

The shortest way to reach divine love is through the love of the Prophet ﷺ, the beloved Messenger of Allah. This goal can be achieved by following him in every aspect of life. Our response to him is required by a basic principle of love: a lover must love everything that the beloved loves. Such staunch commitment to Allah's preferences is the bedrock of loving Allah.

Love of the Prophet ﷺ reveals itself through peacefulness in worship, courtesy in personal relations, politeness in morality, tenderness of heart, radiance of face, spirituality in conversation, and depth of perspective. The only fountain from which all these beauties may be drawn is Muhammad ﷺ.

Indeed, our hearts can fully benefit from the heart of the Prophet ﷺ only when we become moths turning around his light. Mawlânâ Jalaluddin Rumi gives us several examples of how divine love disseminates into the universe. These examples allow us to measure our love of the Prophet:

Innumerable moths jump into fire for the sake of love. They flutter in flame and burn, saying in the language of their state, "You become like me!" ....

The candle flames and weeps. It submits itself to the fire and suffers gravely. It gives out light while dissolving in tears. The candle says: "It is useless to spend gold and silver wildly in order to bring yourself profit. If you want spiritual profit, burn and melt like me!"

The Prophet ﷺ whom we love dearly wept again and again, repeating "My community, my community!" His love and compassion for his community were incomparably stronger than those of a loving and affectionate mother for her children. He was anxious about what his community would be facing on the Day of Judgment, and he suffered much to save his people. He said, "In the way of Allah I was subjected to much suffering that no one had faced before." (Tirmidhi, Qiyamah 34/2472).

The Prophet 🕌 said to the Companions: "Be careful! I am a protection for you on earth while I am alive, and I will continue in my grave. I will keep praying for you to Allah the Almighty, saying 'My community, my community!' until the last trump of doom." (Ali al-Muttaqi, *al-Kanz al-Ummah*, vol. 14, p. 414).

For the sake of our eternal life, we should truly love the Prophet 🕌 more than we love ourselves, since he told us, "A believer will be together with the one he loves." (Bukhari, Adab 96). All Muslims should show loyalty to the Prophet's community because of his love for it.. That loyalty is an indicator of how much we love him.

Here are two counsels from the Prophet 🕌 that we can use as capital to invest toward our worldly and otherworldly wellbeing.

1. "My Lord ordained that I forgive whoever oppressed me (personally). (I advise you to follow me in that.)"[15]

Forgiveness is valuable when one has the ability to punish and retaliate and yet forgives instead. Such behavior manifests love toward the creation for the sake of our love of the Creator. Muslims should be humble enough to decline revenge, leaving transgressors to the trial of Allah on the Day of Judgment. Such acts of forgiveness are acts of pure spiritual merit for mature and decent believers. By continually forgiving others, the faithful person wins forgiveness from Allah.

Hadrat `Umar 🕌 said, "Whoever does not show mercy is not shown mercy. Whoever does not forgive is not forgiven." (Bukhari, *al-Adab al-Mufrad*, p. 415, 371).

---

15. İbrahim Canan, *Hadis Ansiklopedisi*, XVI, 252, no. 5838.

Forgiveness is not attractive to our lower-self. It is therefore a great virtue to forgive for the sake of Allah. Since the value of an act depends upon its difficulty, Allah appreciates our forgiving to the extent of our struggle to forgive.

A man who was weak at overcoming anger asked the Prophet ﷺ to give him advice. The Prophet ﷺ simply said, "Do not get angry!" The man asked the same thing three times.. The Prophet ﷺ gave him the same answer three times. (Bukhari, Adab 76).

The Prophet ﷺ urged his community to develop the habit of forgiveness. He said, "Don't be like the ones who say, 'If people do good to us, we will do good to them. If they do evil to us, we will do evil to them'. Make a practice of being good toward those who do good to you and those who do evil to you, alike!" (Tirmidhi, Birr 63/2007). A Turkish proverb touches on the same point: "Even the simple return a favor for a favor – only the mature return a favor for a slight." Such a practice is in fact a method of spiritual training.

When an enemy receives a favor in return for an evil act, that person's heart may soften and hostility may cease. Through an act of forgiveness, an uncommitted person may become a friend – and an ordinary friend may become a close friend.

It is said in the Qur'an:

The good and the evil are not alike. Repel (evil) with that which is better, and then he between whom and you was enmity may become like an intimate friend. (Fussilat, 41/34).

Ibn 'Abbas ﷺ interpreted this verse thus: "The phrase *"what is better"* refers to being patient in times of anger, and to forgiving when one is done evil. Allah the Almighty saves those who can manage such a practice, making their enemies surrender and become friends." (Bukhari, Tafsir 41/1).

History witnesses that humanity has benefited much from the virtue of forgiveness. It has led human beings away from evil, injustice, and tyranny, and awakened many from moral ignorance.. One such incident occurred when the Prophet ﷺ conquered Mecca and declared amnesty for the people of the city. He addressed the populace, who gathered around the Ka`bah, "O people of Mecca! What do you reckon that I am going to do about you?"

They replied, "We expect nothing but good from you. You are a brother with a generous heart and also the son of a brother to us. We believe you care about us!.."

The Prophet ﷺ said, "I say to you what the Prophet Joseph said to his brothers: '(*There shall be) no reproof against you this day; Allah may forgive you, and He is the most merciful of the merciful*'. (Yusuf, 12/92)."

When the Prophet had the chance of holding captive the idol-worshippers of Mecca who had tyrannized the Muslims for many years, he instead forgave ten and set them free.[16] The hearts of the idol- worshippers softened, and many embraced Islam in the end.

❖

While Zainab, the beloved daughter of the Prophet, was emigrating to join her father in Medina, someone called Habbar ibn Aswad rushed at her with a spear. Zainab fell on a rock and was wounded severely. She was pregnant, and miscarried. At length she died because of the injuries she suffered. Habbar, who had committed many other crimes against Muslims, ran away when the Muslims conquered Mecca.

Some time later, while the Prophet was sitting in a council circle with the Companions, Habbar came into his presence. He

---

16. Ibn Hisham, IV, 32; Waqidi, II, 835; Ibn Saad, II, 142-143.

embraced Islam and begged pardon for his earlier crimes. The Prophet forgave him, and further, forbade the Companions to harm him because of his earlier acts.[17] Allah says in the Qur'an:

Take to forgiveness, and enjoin good, and turn away from the ignorant. (`Araf, 7/99).

The Prophet used to forgive all personal offenses against him. However, he also used to make sure that justice was done if crimes were committed against the public. In such cases, he permitted no one to intervene in the punishment of the offender. If an offense is directed toward the public, then the rights of the people must be protected. If a public offense is forgiven, such an act opens the way for more injustice.

It was one of the most distinctive attributes of the Prophet to forgive for the sake of Allah. He forgave even those who outraged and tortured him while he was delivering the message of Allah – he would pray that Allah lead them to the true path and honor them with Islam. The Prophet was once stoned by the ignorant idol-worshippers of Taif. Angel Gabriel came to him declaring that he was ready to destroy those people, upon request. The Prophet replied,: "No! I only wish to have people of their generation worship Allah alone, not idols." (Bukhari, Bad` al-Khalq 7; Muslim, Jihad 111). And the people of Taif embraced Islam before long – due, perhaps, to this prayer of the Prophet .

✤

Someone called Mistah, a poor man given much financial help by Hadrat Abu Bakr, joined the evil people who slandered Hadrat A'ishah, Abu Bakr's daughter. What Mistah did troubled Abu Bakr greatly. The slander victim was the mother of the community and

---

17. Waqidi, *al-Maghazi*, II, 857-858.

the wife of the Prophet, as well as his own beloved child. Abu Bakr was so annoyed by Mistah's ingratitude that he vowed not to help him further. Mistah and his family became destitute. Then the Qur'anic verse was revealed:

"...Do you not love that Allah should forgive you?" (Nur, 24/22).

Upon hearing this, Abu Bakr said: "Yes, I definitely want to be forgiven!" He repented his anger, and returned to offering Mistah financial support (Bukhari, Maghazi 34; Muslim, Tawbah 56).

It is Allah who is the ultimate forgiver. Muslims take pleasure in forgiving to the extent that Allah's love is in their hearts. Those who wish to taste union with the divine being need to forgive for Allah's sake. The spiritual victory goes to those who willingly forgive people who treat them unjustly..

2. The Messenger of Allah constantly counseled his community, "My Lord ordained that I enjoin the right and prevent the wrong. (I advise you to follow me in that.)"

To enjoin the right and prevent the wrong is the most important service anyone can perform for humanity. It is the result of loving creation for the sake of its Creator. What human beings need most is to find salvation in faith. Calling people to the true path is, therefore, a sacred duty. This duty is called "the profession of the prophets." Allah the Almighty says in the Qur'an:

Most certainly then We will question those to whom (the Messengers) were sent, and most certainly We will also question the Messengers. (Surah `Araf, 7/6).

Prophet Muhammad ﷺ committed himself to calling to the true path. During his last Pilgrimage to the Ka`bah, the "Farewell

Pilgrimage," he asked the people whether he had properly done his job. As we are his community, his job is also our job.

It is said in the Qur'an:

And who speaks better than he who calls to Allah while he himself does good, and says: I am surely of those who submit? (Fussilat, 41/33).

And from among you there should be a party who invite to good, who enjoin the right and forbid the wrong, and these it is that shall be successful. (Al `Imran, 3/104).

The Prophet ﷺ said, "I swear by Allah that it is much better for you that Allah guide a man to Islam through you than that you should own red camels [the most valuable property at that time]." (Bukhari, Ashab al-Nabi 9).

How happy are the faithful who deserve this reward! The Prophet ﷺ, again, said, "The one who calls to the right path gets as much spiritual reward as all those who follow, without any reduction in the reward of those who follow." (Muslim, `Ilm 16).

The reward accruing to sincere acts for Allah's sake gets bigger and bigger, just as a snowball becomes an avalanche. Therefore it is our duty to warn nonbelievers and also ignorant believers who are not strong in faith, and urge them to find the right path. This would, of course, be the best help for them, and we may expect blessing for calling them to the way of Allah.

Our efforts to call to the way of Allah are, indeed, an indicator of our sincerity in faith. The Prophet ﷺ says, "If any of you should witness an evil act, let him amend it by his hand. If he cannot, let him amend it by his words. If he still cannot, let him feel displeasure in his heart. The last option is the lowest level of faith." (Muslim, Iman 78).

There are severe warnings for those who are oblivious about calling to the true path. The Prophet 🵖 said in this regard, "I swear by Allah the Almighty who endowed me with my life, that you will either enjoin the right and prevent the wrong, or you will draw down the wrath of Allah. Afterwards you will pray Allah to forgive you, but your prayers will not be answered." (Tirmidhi, Fitan 9).

Yet one should be careful about the rules and principles of calling to the way of Allah. One's efforts, otherwise, may bring disservice to faith rather than service. We must be deeply knowledgeable about the meaning of what is right and good. Any call by the ignorant is bound to have mistakes in both form and content.

The basis of a good call is knowledge and a pure heart. Without knowledge and wisdom one cannot be successful, just as a host cannot offer an empty cup to a guest.

It is not a good idea for someone who has moral failings and suffers from selfishness to try to call people to Allah. Such a person may cause worse results. To transmit this religion well, one needs a humble heart adorned with the wisdom of the Qur'an and a pleasant face reflecting the smiling nature of Islam. One should be a symbol of what is good and right and speak the language of the heart.

Calling to the way of Allah should be accompanied by kindness and beneficence as well as Islamic courtesy. Such treatment will make one's audience ready to receive the message. We all respond well to good treatment and respectful behavior.

The person who calls to the way of Allah is supposed to turn a blind eye to the past failings or mistakes of those addressed, since the audience has an unconditional right to learn what the message is. The caller should not exclude anyone from the message, bearing in mind that many trees blossom out of stones, and that the grace of Allah is boundless.

The Prophet ﷺ did not close the door of the message of Islam to people like Habbar ibn Aswad, who caused the death of his daughter Zaynab; or 'Ikrimah ibn Abi Jahl, who performed all kinds of hostile acts until the conquest of Mecca; or Wahshi, who martyred the Prophet's uncle, Hadrat Hamza; or Hind, wife of Abu Sufyan, who savagely chewed on Hadrat Hamza's liver. It doesn't matter if the person invited to Islam is as strong in blasphemy as Pharaoh: he or she may not be excluded from the call to the way of Allah. When Allah the Almighty asked Prophet Moses to visit Pharaoh, who pretended to be a god himself, He instructed him to call Pharaoh to the right way gently.

Whoever calls to Islam must preach the greatness of Allah's mercy and compassion to sinful people who have despaired of them. It is said in the Qur'an:

Say: O my servants who have acted extravagantly against their own souls! Do not despair of the mercy of Allah; surely Allah forgives the faults altogether; surely He is the Forgiving, the Merciful. And return to your Lord time after time, and submit to Him before there comes to you the punishment: then you shall not be helped. (Zumar, 39/53-4).

We need good and wise words to call to Allah those people who feel themselves trapped in a sinful life.

Thus it is a duty of believers to do our best, without negligence, to call people to the way of Allah. As to the results of our efforts, we must resign ourselves to the will of Allah. We should not undertake this work egotistically, thinking to rely upon "soul-saving" for our own salvation. We must simply endeavor to make the principles of Islam known to all.

It is the art of the heart to read the meaning and mystery of creation. Allah the Almighty has expressed much wisdom through His creatures, and He has created them in limitless numbers. The universe is a spectacular classroom for those with the gifts and the readiness to learn. Such Friends of Allah as Mawlana Jalaluddin Rumi and Yunus Emre have been star pupils in this classroom. They gained divine wisdom from the mysteries of this universe, and with what they learned, they continue to sprinkle spiritual perfume upon yearning hearts.

Our Lord opened up the whole universe as a book from which all of us may learn.

Our Lord manifests many lessons, in all beings, for hearts that can feel and eyes that can see. His manifestation attracts our attention to the wisdom of giving.

A bee has a life of 45 days, on average. During that time it produces honey, but the amount it makes is perhaps a hundred times more than what it needs.. The bee's life is not for itself, but for others.

A plum tree's fruit contains the seed by which it keeps its species alive. Plum trees, however, produce many more plums than are necessary for reproduction. The tree fruits so that others may benefit from it.

These are among the wonderful examples of altruism displayed in creation by our Lord.

Our Lord offers us the plane tree to tell us what this worldly life is about. The enormous plane tree loses its leaves in winter; and in doing so, shows us silently that death is real. In spring, it shows us that rising from death is also real. The plane tree bears no fruit, and is useless for timber. When its life is done, it can only be used for firewood. That means its legacy is small. It silently warns us: "Be aware, and understand that you are finite beings. Do not be as fruitless as I am!"

We should try to be like the olive tree, and gain skills that give maximum benefit to others. The olive tree has no mighty trunk, yet it starts bearing fruit within the year it is planted, and it keeps on bearing indefinitely. The rose, too, tells us silently: "I am always smiling with my color and scent, although I endure thorns in my body. I advise the same to you!"

Prosperity without giving to others, health and status or education without gratitude – all this is like being a dead plane tree. It is important for believers to be like fruit trees, and to work to be more fruitful all the time.

People of faith should ask themselves, "How much of my thinking and acting are self-centered? How much do I think about other people in need? How many sacrifices do I make? What might the bee, the rose, the plum tree, and the olive tree mean to me?"

As a human being is more highly honored than a bee or a tree, we should endeavor to be more beneficial to creation than a bee or a tree. The human being is the most highly honored of the creatures of Allah. We ought, therefore, to serve ourselves once, but others a thousand times. It is said in the Qur'an:

...And they ask you as to what they should spend. Say: What you can spare. (Baqarah, 2/219).

May our Lord help us duly to know and thank Allah for all beneficence, and may we be, throughout our lives, attuned to the will of Allah. May Allah help us to be people from whom others benefit in all aspects, in our words, in our acts, and in our attitudes, and may He include us among the sincerely faithful. May Allah help us to think and to act in harmony with His will!

Amin...

CHAPTER 4

Love For The Prophet's Household

The Prophet's Household had the privilege of closely witnessing the beauty of his face, the eloquence of his
words, and the decency of his behavior. They were especially dear to the Prophet ﷺ for he trained them himself,
both in acts and in attitudes.

LOVE FOR THE PROPHET'S HOUSEHOLD

> The Prophet ﷺ said: "Love Allah because He has treated you with beneficence. Love me because you love Allah, and love my family because you love me!"
> (Tirmidhi, al-Manaqib, 31/3789).

Love and friendship

Love and friendship grow out of feeling and acting together. The more things are shared between people, the more friendship and love they feel. Love manifests fully when the lover sees his or her attributes in the beloved.

Allah the Almighty loves those servants in whom He sees His beautiful attributes, and He allows them to come closer to Him. Hadrat Jacob loved his son Hadrat Joseph most dearly of all his twelve children because he saw the reflection of his own feelings, thoughts, skills, and qualities in Joseph. Among Muslims, those in whom the qualities of the Prophet ﷺ were reflected most clearly, and were therefore most beloved, are his family members, the people of the Prophet's household.

The Prophet's Household had the privilege of closely witnessing the beauty of his face, the eloquence of his words, and the decency of his behavior. They were especially dear to the Prophet ﷺ for he trained them himself, both in acts and in attitudes.

These glorious People of the House paid a heavy price, heart and soul, throughout their lives in their worthiness of the Prophet's love. They passed through the path of suffering where the Prophet ﷺ had gone before. People do pay the price of their loves, particularly those who love dearly, and the heaviest price paid in this transient world is the price of loving Allah. The Household were the most privileged payers of this price. Great was their commitment, and great was their spiritual ecstasy.

The Household of the Prophet (Ahl al-Bayt)

Ahl al-Bayt means the People of the House – that is, the house of the Prophet, the Glory of Existence. They are the honorable people who were educated most directly by the Prophetic wisdom and morality. They are the masters of the Muslim community, a monument of sincerity and commitment to the Prophet ﷺ.

The term *Ahl al-Bayt,* the Household, is primarily used for the family members of the Prophet ﷺ, and in this sense includes the Prophet ﷺ and his extended family – Ali, Ja`far,`Aqil, `Abbas and their families – may Allah be pleased with them all. As it is an obligation for Muslims to pronounce the formula calling Allah's benediction upon the Prophet ﷺ, so also it is an obligation for us to pay homage and express love for the Household.

It is a natural for lovers to love whatever reminds them of their beloved. Such love may even extend to the beloved's belongings, habits, and familiar places. When we love somebody, we remember the one we love whenever we observe similar style and behavior in other people, and so we invite such people into our circle. The intensity of this phenomenon depends upon the intensity of our love. If we love someone deeply, that person's way of dressing, sitting, or walking finds a place in our heart. Muslims' fondness for visiting the honorable robe of the Prophet ﷺ or clippings of his blessed beard is a particular example of this effect of love.

Love of Allah is the zenith of love. Next in dignity is love of the Prophet ﷺ, our master, for whom the universe was created in the beginning. Those who take the love of the Prophet ﷺ deeply into themselves also love his Household, and follow their honorable ways.

Zayd ibn Arqam ﷺ said: "One day, the Prophet ﷺ addressed us while standing by the fountainhead called Hum somewhere between Mecca and Medina. He first praised Allah the Almighty and gave us some counsel saying, 'O people! I too am a human being. And the envoy of my Lord, the angel Gabriel, will come for me soon. I will accept the invitation of my Lord and go. I am leaving two important things with you. The first is the Book of Allah, which is the glorious guide leading you to the right path. Follow it earnestly.' The Prophet ﷺ gave us some more advice about following the Qur'an, and then continued, "I also leave with you my household. Fear Allah and show respect to my household! Fear Allah and show respect to my household!'"

The listeners asked Zayd who the members of the Household were, and whether the wives of the Prophet ﷺ were included among them. Zayd answered, "His wives are also the Household. Yet the crucial members of the Household are Ali, `Aqil, Ja`far, and the family of `Abbas, who are all forbidden to take alms." (Muslim, al-Fada'il al-Sahabah, 36).

Salman is one of us

In addition to the biological members of the Prophet's Household, there are also its spiritual members. Salman al-Farisi ﷺ, though a foreigner, so naturally manifested the character of a Muslim that the people of Mecca and Medina both claimed Salman as a member of their respective communities. Upon hearing their discussion of Salman, the Prophet ﷺ exalted his position, saying: "Salman is one of us, one of my household." (Ibn Hisham, III, Waqidi, II, 446-7; Ibn Saad, IV, 83; Ahmad, II, 446-7; Haythami, VI, 130).

This statement of the Prophet ﷺ shows that the basic condition for being counted among the Household is commitment to Islam and a pious life. The door is open for others, outside the relations of blood and marriage, to become members of the Prophet's Household – and this is the highest position a Muslim can reach.

The story of Mu`adh ibn Jabal, who is renowned for his commitment, is a good example. One day, the Prophet ﷺ accompanied Mu`adh to the outskirts of Medina. He was sending him off to Yemen to serve as governor. Hadrat Mu`adh was riding, while the Prophet ﷺ was walking. He gave him some advice, and then said, "Mu`adh! Perhaps you will not see me again. Perhaps you will visit my tomb when you return!" Hearing this, Mu`adh began to weep. "Don't cry!" the Prophet ﷺ said. Then he turned toward Medina and remarked: "Among the people, those who are closest to me are those who fear Allah and are most committed in their faith."[18]

Elsewhere the Prophet ﷺ, the honor of the universe, again specified the basic condition for affiliating with him by saying that "My associates are those who are most committed in their faith." (Abu Dawud, al-Fitan, 1/4242). Another such example is `Usamah ibn

18. Ahmad, V, 235; al-Haythami, *al-Majmu`a al-Zawa;id,* Bairut 1988, IX, 22.

Zayd ﷺ. One day Ali and `Abbas ﷺ came to the Prophet ﷺ asking whom he loved most among his Household. The Prophet ﷺ said he loved Fatimah, his beloved daughter, most. They said, "O Messenger! We are not asking about women." The Prophet ﷺ replied, "Then the dearest to me among my Household is `Usamah ibn Zayd, who got the blessing of Allah the Almighty and mine as well." (Tirmidhi, al-Manaqib, 40/3819)

The great transmitter of Prophetic traditions, Hakim al-Tirmidhi, reported that the Friends of Allah of later times are believed to be among the Household, spiritually though not biologically, as they are in constant remembrance of Allah, and the Prophet ﷺ was sent by Allah to establish His remembrance in human hearts. (Hakim al-Tirmidhi, *al-Kitab al-Khatm al-Awliya'*, p. 35-6).

Thus we need to have the love and fear of Allah take root in our hearts, and to be in union with Allah and the Prophet ﷺ all the time, so that we may join the spiritual circle of the Household. The Prophet ﷺ said, "People are together with whoever they love." The clear sign of such a position can be observed in one's acts and devotions.

Manners of the Household

The Prophet ﷺ wished the members of his Household, whom he loved dearly, to live a life of commitment in order to be a good example for humanity. He always channeled them toward living a simple, humble, and gentle life, which is the way that leads to salvation in the Hereafter. He always warned them that "the real life is the life of the Hereafter." (Bukhari, al-Riqaq, 1). By this warning he hoped to wean them away from even allowable worldly acts, so as to encourage them to more commitment and to a more present awe of Allah. He was not apprehensive that they might develop an inclination toward the affairs of this world.

The Prophet ﷺ had a special love for his daughter Fatimah. No father could express more love than the Prophet ﷺ did toward Fatimah. We are, therefore, of the opinion that naming a daughter Fatimah will bring blessing to a family and draw it closer to the Prophet ﷺ.

The Prophet ﷺ said, "Fatimah is part of me. Anyone who upsets her, upsets me, and anyone who pleases her, pleases me."[19] He also announced the good news that she would be counted one of the most virtuous women in Paradise.[20]. Yet on the other hand, he warned her not to rely on being his daughter, and to be aware of the Day of Judgment. "O Fatimah! Follow ways which will save you from Hellfire! I do not have the power to save you, but I will be connected to you because you are my kin." (Muslim, al-Iman, 348, 351).[21]

The Prophet ﷺ loved Hadrat Fatimah so much that he wanted the next world for her more than this one. He urged her to engage with worldly life in only the most modest way, and to give away her extra belongings in charity. He always warned her against any inclination toward worldly desires, but encouraged her in things of the spirit.

One day the Prophet ﷺ saw Fatimah wearing a necklace. He said nothing, but Hadrat Fatimah, who was a sensitive and delicate person, upon seeing his face, immediately understood his thought. She immediately went out and sold the necklace and distributed its price, though she herself needed that money. The Prophet ﷺ was very happy when he learned what his daughter had done. (Nasa`i, al-Ziynat, 39).

19. Muslim, al-Fada'il al-Sahabah, 93-96.
20. Ahmad, I, 293.
21. See also Bukhari, at-Tafsir, 26/2; Tirmidhi, at-Tafsir, 27/2.

Hadrat Fatimah was physically weak and fragile. Housework would tire her, and fire-making and cooking were difficult. Sometimes sparks would burn her dress while she was blowing on the fire, and she was troubled by the heavy dust raised when she cleaned the house. Her hands would bruise when she turned the millstone to make flour.

Once some prisoners of war were brought into the presence of the Prophet ﷺ. Hadrat Fatimah asked the Prophet to assign one of them as a housemaid, to help her with the housework. The Prophet ﷺ rejected the idea. "O Fatimah! Fear Allah! Perform the obligatory duties Allah the Almighty has enjoined in full commitment, and do your part in the family. Make your night prayer when in bed by reciting *subhan Allah* ("exalted is Allah") 33 times, *alhamdu lillah* ("praise be to Allah") 33 times, and *Allahu akbar* ("Allah is greater") 34 times – a hundred all together. That will be better for you than having a housemaid." Hadrat Fatimah replied in great commitment and resignation, "I am truly content with Allah the Almighty and His Messenger!" So, the Prophet ﷺ did not assign a housemaid for his daughter whom he loved so much. (Abu Dawud, al-Kharaj, 19-20/2988).

Another narrative on this event reports that the Prophet ﷺ declared,: "I swear by Allah that I cannot assign a housemaid to you while the poor devotees outside my gate (*Ahl al-Suffah*) are tying stones against their bellies to stave off hunger. I am going to spend the ransom I will get for these captives on the *Ahl al-Suffah* " (Ahmad, I, 106).

The Prophet ﷺ accustomed his daughter Fatimah to a humble style of life because she would be the spiritual mother of the Household and of their noble successors – Abdul-Qadir al-Gaylani, Baha'uddin al-Naqshbandi, Ahmad al-Rifa`i, and many more Friends of Allah – as well as serving as a model for Muslim women.

As another example of how the Prophet ﷺ spiritually trained his family, we might examine the 33rd chapter of the Qur'an. Surah Ahzab says:

O wives of the Prophet! you are not like other women. Be on your guard, be not soft in (your) speech, lest he in whose heart is a disease yearn; but speak a word that is good. And stay in your houses, and do not display your finery like the displaying of the ignorance of yore. Keep up prayer, and pay the poor-rate, and respond to Allah and His Messenger. O People of the House! Allah only desires to keep away uncleanness from you, and to purify you a (thorough) purifying. (Ahzab, 33/32-33)

For six months after this revelation, on the way to the mosque each day for morning-prayer, the Prophet ﷺ would stop by the door of Hadrat Fatimah and call out, :"O People of the House! Wake up for prayer! *Allah only desires to keep away uncleanness from you, and to purify you (thorough) purifying*" (Tirmidhi, al-Tafsir, 33/3206).

Again, on nights when they might not be able to wake up for midnight prayers by themselves due to weariness, the Prophet ﷺ would wake Hadrat Ali and Hadrat Fatimah by knocking on their door.

Anas ibn Malik ﷺ said, "I have never seen anyone as gentle toward family members as the Prophet ﷺ was." Such a statement also means that no one could educate family members as effectively as the Prophet ﷺ did. The Prophet ﷺ taught his family to live in full submission to Allah and to be examples to others in this regard. As the Prophet ﷺ was trained directly by Allah the Almighty and became the master of all Messengers of Allah, so the members of his family who were trained directly by him became the masters of all humanity.

The Household was, in truth, made up of people of the heart who melded together around the Prophet ﷺ sent as a mercy to the universe. As the morning wind carries the perfume of the rose garden , so the Household, who grew up under the spiritual training of the Prophet ﷺ, in maturity transmitted his spirituality with great sincerity and submission. As one candle may light countless candles, so these candles of blessing have borne the glory of the Prophet ﷺ to generation after generation.. Those who are fortunate enough to be lit by any of these candles tastes the pleasure of reaching the source of light, Muhammad ﷺ.

Thus the spiritual essence of all Sufi lineages born of Hadrat Ali and Hadrat Abu Bakr must be traced through Ja`far al-Sadiq, the Imam of the Household. Hadrat Imam al-A`zam, the founder of the Hanafi school of jurisprudence, was a prominent student and spiritual child of Ja`far al-Sadiq. Imam al-A`zam tells how he spiritually benefited from Ja`far al-Sadiq: "I would have perished if it had not been for the last two years through which I spent time with Ja`far al-Sadiq."

So the Household has become an exceptional instrument for the transmission of the character and personality of the Prophet ﷺ through the ages.

Love of the Prophet's Household

Allah says in the Qur'an:

...O People of the House! Allah only desires to keep away uncleanness from you, and to purify you a (thorough) purifying. (Ahzab, 33/33).

So, as this verse clearly tells, it is Allah Himself who vindicates the Household.

The Prophet ﷺ loved his family members dearly and also wished his community to love them. He said, "Love Allah because He has treated you with beneficence. Love me because you love Allah, and love my family because you love me!" (Tirmidhi, al-Manaqib, 31/3789).

Abu Bakr ؓ who fully identified himself with the Prophet ﷺ, was also exemplary in expressing respect toward the Household. He would urge the people, "Have love for the Prophet ﷺ, and behave decently to him!. I swear by Allah that the kin of the Prophet ﷺ are dearer to me than my own kin."

Love of the Household is so important that we pray for its members, along with the Prophet ﷺ, in the recitation that accompanies our five daily prayers. This displays the importance of the Household's position in religion. What other set of relatives ever merited such respect?

Imam Shafi`i, the founder of one of the four major schools of jurisprudence, said, "O Household of the Prophet! Love for you is an obligation enjoined in the Qur'an by Allah. The prayer of the one who does not praise you is not acceptable. This should be sufficient for honor!" (Muhammad al-Farsa, *al-Fasl al-Kitab*, p. 522).

The murder that shook the heavens

The murder of Hadrat Husayn ؓ, the grandson of Muhammad ﷺ, whom the Prophet ﷺ loved dearly, kissed kindly, and even put on his shoulder while praying, is one of the greatest atrocities in the history of Islam. This notorious event is still a trauma in Muslim consciousness. All who were involved in this murder received the wrath of Allah.

This atrocious killing was so detested in the Muslim world that the name of the caliph of the time, namely Yazid, has been used by Muslims through the ages as an insult. All Muslims, no matter what denomination or school they follow, have always felt grief for the savage killing of Hadrat Husayn ﷺ. So there is no reason for enmity, and there should be no enmity, between Sunni and Shi`a Muslims on account of the killing of Husayn ﷺ. Yet some provocative troublemakers act as if a basic estrangement exists. Muslims of the two sects should never behave like enemies. Today all Muslims should join together more than ever. As Allah says in the Qur'an

The believers are but brethren... (Hujurat 49/ 10).

Being involved in unreasonable controversies brings no benefit. It harms the unity of the Muslim community and hurts the blessed souls of the past. Sectarian fanaticism, whenever it has arisen among Muslims, has always created damage. Even small frictions offer an opportunity to those who profit from the division the Muslims. Thus it is our duty to be vigilant at all times, not to fall into the trap of disunity, and to keep away from unnecessary arguments.

In order to be successful in this we must establish a third point of common commitment along with the Qur'an and the Prophet tradition, and that is the love of the Household. Such love, which is enjoined by the Prophet ﷺ as well, is a quality that all Muslims should cultivate.

The Ottomans always paid tribute to the Household, and also honored the entire blood lineage of the Prophet ﷺ. They regarded the service of the Household so highly that an office called *Naqib al-Ashraf* (Chief of the Descendants of the Prophet) was established in the Ottoman Empire to protect the dignity of the Household.

We, descendants of blessed ancestors, should enliven our hearts with the love of the Qur'an and of the Household, so that we may be worthy of the love of the Prophet ﷺ. We should take the Prophet ﷺ as an example in our acts and words. Let us identify with him and his *ahl al-bayt*.

O Lord! Please let us have a share of the spirit of the Prophet ﷺ, of his Household and Companions, and of the Friends of Allah!

Amin...

CHAPTER 5

Righteousness and Justice - 1

We should not forget that Allah the Almighty, who orders His servants to observe rights and justice, always supports those who are subjected to injustice. Those who think that they can get away with whatever they do in this worldly life cannot escape kneeling down and trying to explain themselves before Almighty Allah, the judge over all judges..

CHAPTER 5

RIGHTEOUSNESS AND JUSTICE - 1

Islamic ethics include all aspects of human beauty and perfection and take the human soul to the zenith of virtues. They have an exceptional essence, for they are unshakably founded upon rights and justice. This is because the peace of humanity can be ensured only if rights and justice are observed.

So what are rights and justice?

The most general definition is *"to treat everybody and everything according to its due; to judge truthfully; and to behave toward all in a balanced and moderate manner."*

On this definition, to give somebody more than his rightful due is to violate the rights of others, while to give him less than his rightful due is to usurp his rights, that is, to violate justice. People of sincere faith are extremely careful to avoid such a crime. That is, a believer feels compelled to give each human being whatever is rightfully due.

Islam demands justice at every stage of life and in all kinds of situations. Pursuing a life that is pleasing to Allah requires us to observe the balance of rights and justice, for justice occupies a central place among the divine orders and prohibitions. Thus a believer

SUCH A MERCY HE WAS...

must first act justly toward his Creator, then toward other creatures, and finally toward him- or herself.

Accordingly, every believer must observe justice when measuring goods, when judging people, when writing records, and when testifying in court. Additionally, we must pay proper attention to what is due to Allah in our ritual prayers and devotions. We must observe their due form, because that is a right belonging to our Lord. His servants are responsible for them to Him.

The faithful person who organizes life according to this consciousness and the measures of rights and justice reaches the state of *ahsan al-taqwîm,* "the finest design." This is because the observance of rights and justice are among the divine attributes. The Beautiful Name *al-'Adl,* "the Just," indicates that Allah the Almighty is the absolute owner of right and justice, and even that He is right and justice themselves. This exalted Name is always manifesting in this world, but it will be manifest in all its majesty at the divine judgment in the Hereafter. Allah declares in the Noble Qur'an:

We shall set up scales of justice for the Day of Judgment, so that not a soul will be dealt with unjustly in the least, and if there be (no more than) the weight of a mustard seed, We will bring it (to account): and enough are We to take account. (Anbiya'; 21/47).

We should never forget that Allah the Almighty, who orders His servants to observe rights and justice, always supports those who are subjected to injustice. Those who think that they can get away with whatever they do in this worldly life cannot escape kneeling down and trying to explain themselves before Allah the Almighty, the judge over all judges.

We can say that humanity, of all beings, bears the heaviest responsibility regarding rights and justice. The human being is the noblest of creatures and all other beings are placed at our disposal. Consequently, we carry the responsibility for their rights and welfare. This is why humanity is obliged not only to protect its own rights but also the rights of all. We are answerable for the rights of plants, animals, and inanimate things as well as our own.

Among the Friends of Allah we find excellent examples of careful observance of the rights of all. In one account, Bâyazid al-Bistâmî, one of Allah's Friends, rested under a tree and ate a meal, then continued on a journey. After some miles he noticed an ant on his traveling bag. "O my Lord," he exclaimed, "I have separated this ant from its homeland!" He went back to the tree where he had eaten, and left the ant.

The poet Firdawsî has this beautiful couplet in his *Shahnâma*: "Don't trouble the ant hauling a grain of wheat! It too lives its life – and life is sweet."

On the Day of Judgment, all other creatures will be resurrected along with humankind, and will claim the rights that were violated during their lives in this world. This is why it is forbidden to make an animal suffer, to fatigue it unduly, or even to cut the branch of a tree without need. We are allowed to kill harmful animals out of necessity, but even when killing a harmful animal we should not cause unnecessary pain. For example, when trying to protect oneself from a snake, it is proper to dispatch it with a single stroke.

In summary, every person of faith must grasp the true meaning of rights and responsibilities and be extremely careful in establishing justice. For a believer, just conduct in all dealings is among the greatest of virtues. Yet for those who mount the staircase of maturity, there is a virtue even higher than this: forgiveness in justice.

The virtue of forgiveness in justice

Those of sincere faith who reach a broader horizon of vision prefer to respond with forgiveness and mercy instead of demanding justice in their personal affairs. This is because they hope that Allah may treat them in the Hereafter with forgiveness, mercy, kindness, and beneficence instead of justice. Allah praises such good character traits:

If you punish, then punish with the like of that wherewith you were afflicted. But if you endure patiently, verily it is better for the patient. (Nahl, 16/126).

Is not our main objective to receive Allah's kind and generous treatment? This is why virtuous and good servants do not retaliate when they suffer from cruelty and harshness; they do not prefer to punish. They prefer to be patient for the sake of Allah, and overcome their anger. Such servants always take the road of tolerance, and aim at receiving divine mercy themselves through constantly showing mercy to Allah's other servants.

As we have mentioned, for the sake of this principle Abu Bakr ﷺ forgave the person who slandered our mother A'ishah and kept giving him alms (Bukhari, Maghazi, 34; Muslim, Tawbah, 56), encouraged by this Qur'anic verse:

Let not those among you who are endued with grace and amplitude of means resolve by oath against helping their kinsmen, those in want, and those who have left their homes in Allah's cause: let them forgive and overlook. Do you not wish that Allah should forgive you? (....Nûr, 24/22)

And this is why wise people behave according to the guidance of this verse:

The good deed and the evil deed are not alike. Repel the evil deed with one which is better, then lo! he, between whom and you there was enmity (will become) like an intimate friend. (Fussilat, 41/34).

One of the great examples of this morality in the Holy Qur'an is the case of the prophet Joseph 🙼 who suffered a terrible injustice committed by his brothers. Without letting them know his true identity, this great prophet generously offered hospitality and gifts to his brothers when they came to him asking help. Having received all this, they became aware that their benefactor was Joseph. and bore witness to the truth:

They said: "By Allah! indeed has Allah preferred you above us, and we certainly have been guilty of sin!" (Yûsuf, 12/91).

Prophet Joseph 🙼 displayed a great spirit of forgiveness and strengthened his virtue by saying:

This day let no reproach be (cast) on you: Allah will forgive you, and He is the most merciful of those who show mercy! (Yûsuf, 12/92).

Moreover, Joseph blames the Devil, not his brothers, when he says

…Satan had sown enmity between me and my brothers…(Yûsuf, 12/100).

"I was sold as a slave. Thanks to you, the Egyptians also came to know that I am the son of a prophet!" It is Joseph's compliment to his brothers that most displays his virtue. He not only forgave them – he also veiled the cruelty and injustice they had showed him in the past.. This led the erring brothers to frank admiration of the brother they had betrayed.

Based on the high morality of Prophet Joseph, we can say that preferring mercy over justice and forgiving the guilty manifests a whole different level of restoration and guidance. But in order to merit such treatment, the guilty person must be sorry and regretful for his crimes, and understand his faults. We should never forget this. For if the guilty person receives forgiveness even though he does not feel regretful, then forgiving him ceases to be virtuous and becomes a sign of weakness and inability instead.

Whether mercy and forgiveness function successfully depends upon the condition and character of the guilty person. Forgiving an impious and cruel person may encourage that person to continue his course of behavior. If the guilty person is unlikely to amend his conduct when forgiven, then those he has treated unjustly will naturally demand his punishment.

We may forgive the guilty when our personal rights are transgressed. However, public crimes that involve the rights of other people require the full establishment of justice, otherwise impunity will encourage further crimes. All of society may be damaged by such people's cruelty.

Our guide of life, the Messenger of Allah, used to forgive outrageous behavior against his person. Yet he was never tolerant of injustice done to others. He would pursue issues until the people wronged had their rights restored.

This is our measure in observing rights and justice. Only people who practice justice in this fashion will practice it correctly. And if we treat people justly in the first place, we may expect them to treat us justly in return. Whatever peace and happiness are achievable in human life depend on keeping the scales of rights and justice in balance.

Worldly justice is indispensable in securing the order and harmony of societies. However, justice has other implications in the arena of consciousness and feeling that human beings enter in the presence of their Lord. Divine justice follows its own rules.

Struggling with the concept of divine justice has led many astray. We observe that in this world, all people do not have the same opportunities. Some of them are rich, some are poor; some have disabilities at birth, some are healthy; and some live long while others have shorter lives. Since all these things are determined by Allah the Almighty, the disparities might appear to contradict divine justice. Such is the conclusion of rough reasoning and the ignorant heart. However, from the window of faith and wisdom, we may discern something else. Justice is based on the deserving of something.

Justice is involved only if something is deserved!

People were not created because we deserved to be created. The creation of humanity out of nothing is a great divine gift for which there is no proper gratitude. How magnificent a gift it is to appear in the realm of existence from the realm of nonexistence, and within the realm of existence to be created as a human being, the noblest of all creatures, rather than as serpent or a centipede, a stone or a piece of soil or a weed or a leaf. This and many other provisions are simply given to us, free of charge. What price did we pay in order to receive such bounty?

Given this extraordinary situation, to demand "justice" from Allah with a skeptical attitude because of temporary deprivations is to doom oneself to destruction. We are owed nothing. Justice requires deserving something, which means having an intrinsic right to it, earning it by work, or paying a price for it. But what kind of price did we pay for the privilege of being created? What work could entitle us to be human? Nothing, nothing.

Allah the almighty has willed that life shall have two stages, a worldly stage and a second stage in the Hereafter. In the first stage, Allah most clearly manifests himself through the attribute of the Gracious, while in the second, He most clearly manifests himself through the attribute of the Just. It is in the Name of the Gracious that Allah created the universe and human beings, not in the Name of the Just.

All of the wealth acquired by creatures is a gift provided by Allah. Allah is not obliged to provide His creatures with identical gifts. In fact, if any two creatures were equal in all respects, then the existence of one of them would be pointless and absurd. Allah's attribute of perfection *al-Muta`âli,* "Exalted over all," that which transcends even imagination, does not permit the pointless and absurd. Allah the almighty has created all things and ordered them with a precise equilibrium. Allah is indeed free from all faults.

Accordingly, nobody may ask: "What kind of fault did I commit, that I am short?" "Why was I born to ignorant parents instead of educated ones?" "Why was I born poor instead of rich?" All these different situations arise through differences in the manifestation of divine kindness. We may learn this truth from an event of the Age of Felicity.

Tha`labah asked Allah's Messenger for a prayer to become rich. The Prophet ﷺ replied, "O Tha`labah! A little wealth, and thankfulness, is better than a lot of wealth and ingratitude." Then he remarked, "O Tha`labah! Is not my condition of life a good example for you?"

But Tha`labah did not grasp the meaning of this guidance: he insisted on becoming rich. His powerful desire blinded him to the Prophet's warning. So Allah's Messenger prayed that Tha`labah might become rich.. And he became rich – but he fell into ingratitude and discontent. Toward the end of his life, he was deeply regretful. He said on his deathbed, "Would that I listened to the advice of the Prophet ﷺ !" He was terribly sorry that he had followed a desire that had turned his long life into a prison.[22]

This is why one should always keep in mind the Qur'anic verse:

Then you shall be questioned that Day about the joy (you indulged in!). (Takâthur, 102/08).

To be content with that which Allah bestows upon us is both a responsibility and a sign of maturity, for the inequality of the divine bounties is not injustice. Allah the almighty may create one servant in perfect health while creating another with some disability. He may create one with high intellectual capabilities while creating another with less . He may desire some creature to be a snake and make it crawl on the earth, while he may desire another creature to be a bird and make it fly in the air. These differences do not constitute grounds for creatures to object to their own existence.

Animals have just enough intelligence and feeling to maintain their lives, and they are all happy with what they are. They do not have any worry beyond filling their stomachs and satisfying their natural desires. They do not ask why they were not created as human beings! And just as an animal or a plant may not reasonably ask "Why was not I created human?", so people who suffer from some kind of privation, whether disability, illness, or poverty, may not reasonably accuse Allah of injustice.

Moreover, whether small or great wealth would have been better for a person will only be determined at the measuring-scales

---

22. See, Tabarî, *Jâmi'u'l-Bayân*, XIV, 370-372.

in the Hereafter. Smaller resources mean smaller responsibilities, while greater resources mean greater responsibilities.

Whoever cannot grasp the wisdom and mysteries of predestination is best off simply submitting to Allah's discretion. We recall Abu Talhah 🟤 and his wife, Umm Sulaym 🟤, two Companions of the Prophet 🟤. Abu Talhah's son, who was seriously ill, died while Abu Talhah was away from home. Umm Sulaym bathed and shrouded the child's body. When Abu Talhah came home, he asked his wife how their son was doing. Umm Sulaym replied, "His pain is over. I think he feels relieved."

When Abu Talhah was about go out next morning, the intelligent and pious Umm Sulaym said:

"O Abu Talhah! Look at what our neighbor did! When I asked her to give back the property that I lent her, she did not want to return it!"

"How improper that is!" Abu Talhah said.

Then Umm Sulaym said, "O Abu Talhah! Your son was a trust given to you by Allah. He has taken him back." Abu Talhah was shocked at first, and kept silent for a while. Then he recited: "*We belong to Allah, and to Allah we are constantly returning.*" (See, Bukhârî, Janâ'iz 42, Aqîqah 1; Muslim, Adab 23, Fadâ'il as-Sahâba 107).

What a fine example of the awareness that all of Allah's bounties in this world of tests are a trust given to us for but a short time! Such an attitude of contentment and surrender is appropriate both when Allah gives us bounties and when He takes them back.

Indeed, being able to say, following the example of Prophet Abraham 🟤, "*I have surrendered myself to the Lord of the Worlds*" despite all the shifting difficulties of our testing, is one of the major signs of being a praiseworthy servant

O my Lord! May you bestow upon us lives guided by a sincere state of surrender to You! May You make us upholders of rights and justice! May You bestow upon us Your forgiveness and mercy together with rights and justice, and treat us with your forgiveness on the Day of Judgment!

Amin...

CHAPTER 6

Righteousness and Justice - 2

This world is a testing-place. We did not come here without purpose, nor are we left here on our own. ... We are not in this world merely to satisfy our lowest desires. Whoever pursues those desires may easily and unwittingly become a tyrant. In that way we risk our eternal life.

CHAPTER 6

RIGHTEOUSNESS AND JUSTICE - 2

This orderly universe has not come to exist by chance. Neither was it created as a tool for the satisfaction of desires. It was created for a noble purpose, and has been made a place of examination for human beings. Therefore neither the creation of the universe nor the creation of humanity is absurd.

Nothing is created in vain, without wisdom or reason, for another beautiful Name of our Lord is *al-Haqq* – the Right, the Real, the Truth. He is free from doing anything absurd or futile. All things coming from Him are right. The Qur'an declares:

He it is who created the heavens and the earth with truth. (An'âm, 6/73).

Look at the universe as a whole, at humankind, and at other creatures. Each is a wonderful work of art. Their creation displays innumerable wisdoms and lessons, subtle measures and balances. Every person of sound mind should carefully reflect on the manifestation of this divine power.

Allah the Almighty directs our attention to this truth with a warning.

He has raised up the sky and set the measure, so exceed not the measure...(ar-Rahmân, 55/8).

And We created not the heavens and the earth, and all that is between them, for sport. We created them not save with truth; but most of them do not know. (ad-Dukhân, 44/38-39).

Does man think that he is to be left aimless? (Qiyâmah, 75/36).

Have you supposed that We created you in vain, and that you shall not be brought back to Us? (Mu'minûn 23/115)

The noble Qur'an clearly states that this world is a testing-place. We did not come here without purpose, nor are we left here on our own. We have a will that we may use for good or for evil, but our Lord has set some limits, and has commanded us to observe those limits. We are not in this world merely to satisfy our lowest desires. Whoever pursues those desires may easily and unwittingly become a tyrant. In that way we risk our eternal life.

In fact, servanthood means observing the limits set by Allah. By observing those limits, humanity saves itself from divine chastisement. Whoever breaks them has prepared his own punishment, and therefore has tyrannized himself. It must not be forgotten that the opposite of justice is tyranny.

The opposite of justice is tyranny

In the noble Qur'an, Allah Almighty notes as attributes of humanity:

"...Lo! he (man) has proved a tyrant and a fool." (Ahzâb, 33/72)

Violent ignorance, *jahiliyyah*, is one of the major causes leading to injustice and oppression. The opposite of the *jahiliyyah* mentioned in the Noble Qur'an is knowledge, `*ilm*.

True knowledge is that which leads humanity to the recognition of Allah – that is, to our knowing Allah the Almighty in our hearts. Therefore, just as ignorance destines humanity to injustice, so knowledge directs us to goodness, justice, and truth.

The core and origin of truth is Allah the Almighty. Right and truth are made known to us by the creator and possessor of the cosmos. In the Noble Qur'an, Allah tells us:

...Say: The guidance of Allah is guidance indeed, and we are commanded to surrender to the Lord of the Worlds. (An'âm, 6/71).

Remaining indifferent to the commands and prohibitions of Allah and His Messenger, our guides to endless happiness is a bad idea. Whoever does that, tyrannizes himself. The gravest injustice is willfully to remain blind to ultimate truths. Every injustice defines its own punishment. The punishment corresponding to a crime committed against ultimate truths is *an endless chastisement*. Thus failing to keep faith with Allah destines one to Hell forever, because it is the gravest injustice and oppression against all the bounties of one's Lord.

Although injustice evidently causes others to suffer, ultimately it leads whoever commits it into a terrible chastisement. The unjust harm themselves most. This is why in the Qur'an we frequently find the expression "*those who tyrannize themselves.*"

Rûmî ﷺ says of justice and injustice: "What is justice? It is watering fruit trees. What is injustice? It is watering briars," and "A person with no notion of justice is like a she-goat who suckles a baby wolf."

That is, the injustice such a person feeds will lead to his own destruction. It destines him to collapse and disappear.

History bears witness that those who violate the rights of others for their private temporary interests only prepare their own dreadful ends. Finally they are destroyed by their own works. Thus, even if it is quite difficult, one must always uphold justice and support the right.

In the simplest language, injustice means to make people suffer without any good reason.

Despite the fact that human beings have the noblest place in all of creation, we neglect our elevated worth and dignity to chase after transitory pleasures, lowly desires, and fleeting passions. In this way, through sin and rebellion against the divine order, people destine themselves to endless chastisement. But who shall be held responsible for this situation?

The capacity to act justly and mercifully toward others is first and foremost the result of our acting justly and mercifully toward ourselves. And our best guide in reaching this end is the Prophet Muhammad ﷺ.

The best example of justice

Our Lord sent our Prophet ﷺ to illustrate ideal human behavior, and in this way clarified the divine commands and prohibitions. The praiseworthy life of the Prophet ﷺ demonstrates the intentions of Allah for human beings through living human examples. Our noble religion, Islam, is a religion of real life as it may actually be lived in the best manner. Its principles differ from human worldviews which are purely theoretical and cannot be put into practice. Thus the understanding of justice in Islam, although exalted, is also very concrete. Responsibilities are clear.

When the Prophet ﷺ commanded his community to do something, he and his relatives were primarily responsible for applying that command. When he prohibited something, he and his relatives were primarily responsible for abstaining from it. In matters of justice, he did not assume any privilege, nor did he grant privileges to wealthy or influential people. The life of the Prophet Muhammad 🕊 is full of examples of virtuous behavior that make one marvel. Here are a few.

Even if it were my daughter Fâtimah…

During the Age of Felicity, a woman of a noble family of the Banu Makhzûm clan committed theft, and the victim invoked the law against her. Relatives of the woman sought someone to intercede with the Prophet 🕊 so that she might escape punishment. Finally they decided to send `Usâmah ibn Zayd 🕊, who was one of the dearest Companions of the Prophet 🕊. `Usamah went to the Prophet 🕊 and asked whether she might be spared. The Prophet 🕊 listened, and his face changed color. He looked at his beloved Companion reproachfully and asked, "Are you arguing for the cancellation of one of Allah's limits?"

Hearing this, `Usamah 🕊 became utterly regretful. He apologized and said, "O Messenger of Allah! Please pray to Allah for my forgiveness." (Bukhârî, Maghâzî, 53; Nasâ`î, Qat' al-Sâriq, 6, VIII, 72-74).

Then the Prophet 🕊 stood up and announced, "Nations before you were destroyed for the following reason: When somebody with a noble family or a higher rank committed theft, they used to leave him free, but when some poor and alone committed theft, they would punish him immediately. By Allah, if Fâtimah, the daughter of Muhammad, were to commit theft, I would cut off her hand!" (Bukhârî, Anbiyâ', 54; Muslim, Hudûd, 8, 9).

In the Noble Qur'an, Allah says:

"*O you who believe! Be staunch in justice, witnesses for Allah, even though it be against yourselves or (your) parents or (your)*" *kindred, whether (the case concern) the rich or the poor, for Allah is nearer unto both (them you are). So follow not passion, lest you lapse (from truth)..."* (an-Nisâ 4/135)

This episode clearly shows that our Prophet, whose whole life was a kind of explanation of the Qur'an, stood for the rule of law and a respect for the demands of justice even if his own family were to be involved. He certainly rejected granting privileges to people of social influence.

Upholding justice

Even before he was entrusted with the mission of prophethood, Muhammad ﷺ participated in a Meccan civic association known as the Alliance of the Virtuous (*hilf al-fudûl*). This Alliance was established to make justice predominate in business and social life. The group used to help foreigners whose rights were violated and who (through lack of social connections) were unable to insist on their due. It would work to extract from the powerful what was due to the poor, and to restore respect for the rights of the poor.

This sensitivity regarding the implementation of rights and justice can be seen throughout the Prophet's life. One catches a glimpse of it in the following Prophetic sayings:

"....Any society in which a poor man cannot receive his rightful due without being hurt cannot prosper long..." (Ibn Mâja, Sadaqât, 17).

"...How should Allah purify a society (from sins) where the rights of the poor are not extracted from the powerful?" (Ibn Mâja, Fitan, 20).

"On the Day of Judgment, out of all the people, the dearest and closest to Allah will be just rulers. And on the Day of Judgment, out of all the people, the most unlovable and distant from Allah will be unjust rulers." (Tirmidhî, Ahkâm, 4/1329; Nasâ`î, Zakâh, 77)

Again, in the last teaching reported from him, when the Prophet ﷺ was about to depart from this world, he said: "Beware the designated prayers! Be careful about the designated prayers. And be fearful of Allah regarding the rights of those who are under your protection." (Abû Dâwûd, Adab, 123-124/5156; Ibn Mâja, Wasâyâ, 1).

Obstruction of justice: a share of Hell

The pride of the universe, our Prophet Muhammad ﷺ, declared:

"I am only a human being. You come to me asking decisions regarding issues in contention among you. It may happen that one of you is more talented in presenting his evidence and making his case than others. And I may decide in favor of him, based on what I hear. However, if I have decided in favor of anybody based on deceptive evidence, I have allocated that person a share of Hell." (Bukhârî, Shahâdât, 27; Muslim, `Aqidah, 4)

Indeed, some people may cover up their unjust actions and convince people of their innocence through mental acuteness and an ability to speak effectively. Let them not think that they will get away with their crimes! Even if they deceive the courts of this world, in the divine court of the Hereafter everything will be known, and rights will be restored to the defrauded. Such an awful situation in the Hereafter is much more terrible than anything one might experience in this world.

Therefore, anyone who asks the judge for justice must search his conscience as to whether he is truly right in that case.

The issue of justice is important not only in some dimensions of life, but in all of them. It must be implemented in business, in education, and in issues concerning the environment, as well as within the family.

Justice among one's children

To discriminate in favor of sons and against daughters is disrespectful of Allah's decree, and a sign of weak faith and weak Islam.

It is common knowledge that daughters have been deprived of many of their rights and suffered various oppressions. It is totally unjust and tyrannical to regard gender as criterion of superiority, since Allah declares that the only criterion of superiority is *taqwa* – reverent consciousness and carefulness toward Allah.

One of the Companions of the Prophet ﷺ was in a meeting with the Prophet ﷺ. When his little son ran in, he embraced him and put him on his lap. After a while, his little daughter came in too. The Companion bade her sit down next to him. Noticing this, the Prophet ﷺ said: "Should not you observe justice between your children?"

Thus he indicated that one must not discriminate between a son and a daughter on the basis of their gender. One must not prefer one over the other simply on this basis.[23]

Nû`mân ibn Bashîr ﷺ relates:

My father took me to the Prophet ﷺ and said, "I have given a slave that I owned to this son of mine."

The Prophet ﷺ asked: "Have you given the same to your other children?"

23. Tahâwî, *Sharhu Ma'âni'l-Âthâr*, Beirut 1987, IV, 89; Beyhakî, *Shuab*, VII, 468; Haythamî, VIII, 156.

My father said, "No, I have not."

And the Messenger of Allah said, "Then change your decision about this gift." (Bukhârî, Hibah 12, Shahâdât 9; Muslim, Hibât 9-18).

Distributing rights carefully to those who are entitled

After the victory at Khaybar, the Prophet ﷺ used to send Abdullah ibn Rawâhâ there to handle tax collection. Each time, Abdullah ﷺ would carefully estimate the quantity of dates to be levied and would collect the relevant amount of tax.

Certain Jews who farmed at Khaybar were unhappy with Abdullah's estimation, and tried to bribe him to change the levy. They collected their wives' jewelry and offered it to Abdullah, saying, "All this might be yours if you give us a break on the tax!"

Abdullah replied, "I don't like you, because of many wicked actions. But I swear by Allah that my dislike will not prevent me from treating you with justice. Now you are offering me a bribe. But taking bribes is forbidden: we don't do that."

When these Jews understood that they could not bribe Abdullah ﷺ, they appreciated his integrity. They said, "Here are the justice and truthfulness that keep the heavens and the earth in running order." (Muwatta', Musâqât, 2).

Allah says:

O you who believe! Be steadfast witnesses for Allah in equity, and let not hatred of any people seduce you that ye deal not justly. Deal justly, that is nearer to reverence. .... (Mâ'idah, 5/ 8)

How great is our religion, which commands strict observance of justice even toward those who oppose it! A conscious Muslim always respects the right and complies with the requirements of justice, since he keeps in mind that if he commits injustice, even against a nonbeliever, he will be held responsible for it. In fact, in a prophetic tradition the Messenger of Allah said, "Beware of the curse of the oppressed, for there is no veil between his curse and Allah." (Bukhârî, Zakâh 41, 63, Maghâzî 60, Tawhîd 1; Muslim, Îmân 29, 31).

Here is another historical example of the observance of rights and of just treatment offered to non-Muslims.

In the early days of Islam, the city of Hims was under Muslim protection. When the Muslims heard that the Byzantine military was marching toward them, they immediately returned the tax that they had collected from the inhabitants of Hims. They said, "Since we are under military attack now, we are not able to protect you. We only collected these taxes from you in exchange for protecting you. Now you are free to do whatever you want."

The people of Hims said, "We swear by Allah that your government and justice are better for us than the oppression and injustice we suffered under our earlier government. We shall defend the city under your governor's command."

The Jewish and Christian population of other cities that had signed pacts with the Muslims chose to act in the same way. In the end, when the Muslim military won victory, these citizens opened up their cities to the returning Muslims and welcomed their government. They went on living in peace and paying their taxes.[24]

The Muslim military established this tradition of justice not only in Hims, but also in all the towns it originally conquered, when it had to withdraw later on. And the tradition continued. For example, in the Turkish era, when Pleven was conquered by European

24. Balâzûrî, *Futûhu'l-Buldân,* Beirut 1987, s. 187.

forces, Gâzi Osman Pasha returned the taxes that had been collected from the Christian people of Pleven. It was well understood that the tax had existed to pay for their protection.

❀

It is because of such sensitive measures that many non-Muslim thinkers throughout history have appreciated the greatness of the justice taught by Islam. Indeed, when the French revolutionaries were faced with drawing up a Declaration of the Rights of Man in 1789, they did research into all the legal systems of the world. Lafayette, who was then a member of the commission, studied Islamic law. He is reported to have exclaimed, "O glorious Arab! You discovered true justice!"

Justice is the main pillar that upholds societies and keeps states functioning. One old proverb says, "An unbeliever may prosper; but a tyrant will not." Another says, "Justice underlies rule." It is true that nations and states function thanks to governors who possess might and power. However, might and power are acceptable to people only to the extent that they reflect justice. Might without right becomes oppression. Indicating this, Abû Bakr ﷺ said, "Justice without power is impotence. Power without justice is tyranny." That is, power must be bound by justice to be useful, but justice must be delivered by power to be effective.

In *Kutadgu Bilig*, Yûsuf Has Hâcip says, "Injustice is like fire: it destroys whatever it approaches. Justice is like water: it feeds wherever it flows." If the water of justice cannot rescue a society that is burning with the fire of oppression, that water has lost its purity, its fluidity, and its essential character. Any system of justice that is incapable of answering the cries of the oppressed is like polluted water.

When, after the passing of the Prophet, Abû Bakr ﷺ was elected to be caliph, he announced his office to the people with admirable modesty. "O people! I am chosen as caliph even though I am not the best person among you. If I carry out my duties properly, please help me in this cause. If I do wrong, please show me the right path…" (Ibn-i Sa'd, III, 182-183; Suyûtî, *Târîkhu'l-Khulafâ*, s. 69, 71-72; Hamîdullah, *Islâm Peygamberi*, II, 1181).

It follows from the spirit of this declaration that it is incumbent upon Muslims to support just governors, and to warn them without hesitation when they do something wrong.

Resistance to injustice and oppression

The Prophet ﷺ said, "The best jihad is to speak the truth before an unjust ruler." (Abû Dâwûd, Malâhim, 17; Tirmidhî, Fitan, 13). This is because where truth is not spoken, lies prevail. To remain quiet when it is time to defend the right is to turn yourself into a silent devil. To remain quiet before an unjust person is to worship him as an idol.

The people around Pharaoh who encouraged him to claim divinity and demand *"Am I not your lord most high?"* acted like devils despite having the form of human beings. Since they supported Pharaoh's oppression, they were destined to share his disappointment. Fawning on oppressors for the sake of worldly gain is a cause of permanent abasement.

Those whose hearts support the right are blessed by the power of the right. Firmly supported by the right, such people support it in return. It is they who offer resistance to oppressors.

Thus Hasan al-Basrî did not remain silent against the oppression of Hajjâj the Tyrant, whose injustice is well-known. Hasan, taking all kinds of risks, declared the truth, and distributed that which was rightfully due. And Imam al-A`zam Abû Hanîfah, who did not wish to support the unjust policies of the caliph Ja'far Mansûr in any way, rejected his appointment to be chief qadi of Baghdad.

Words of truth are the voice of faith. Telling the truth and distributing what is rightly owed are among the marks of mature people of faith. As long as there people who do these things, the roads to tyranny will be closed.

Those who, following base desires, commit or support oppression must know well that lies and force win only temporary victories. Eternal victory is beyond them, for the destiny of oppression is to disappear. Since rejecting what is true and violating the measures of right and justice means opposition and rebellion against Allah the exalted, unjust people are doomed sooner or later to encounter chastisement by divine power.

The history of oppression and injustice are full of examples of the manifestation of divine vengeance. In this regard, the noble Qur'an says:

...And never did We destroy communities unless the folk thereof were unjust. (Qasas, 28/59). [s.17]

Some people cling to brute force because tyranny seems brilliant at the beginning...but only at the beginning. History shows us repeatedly the darkness at the end. Justice, on the other hand, may be difficult to get started, yet its end is bright and peaceful.

A Muslim who follows justice – everywhere, always, and for everybody – gains the love of Allah and His servants, and reaches nobility and happiness in both worlds. But those who depart from justice for the sake of lowly desires can receive nothing. Even if they gain deceitful and ephemeral benefits, these yield nothing but damage, regret, and disappointment at the end.

May our Lord protect our hearts from bending toward tyranny for the sake of temporary advantage. May He count us all among His happy and fortunate servants who are able to live according to the principles of right and justice, and who enter the Divine Presence with a peaceful mind!

Amin...

CHAPTER 7

Responsibility

A responsibility of empathy linked to religious solidarity is very important. Despite our concrete separateness, Muslims are meant to consider each other as limbs of a single body, all depending on the same heart. Just as pain suffered by one limb is felt throughout the body, so the pain of any suffering Muslim is a trial of conscience for all of us.

RESPONSIBILITY

Human beings are the noblest of creatures and the most precious ornament of the universe. Allah the Almighty has provided humanity with many bounties and capabilities that He did not give to other creatures. In return for these, Allah made human beings responsible beings.

Allah the exalted has placed in us tendencies toward immorality as well as inclinations to reverent consciousness and carefulness toward Him. And He has granted us the free will to choose between the two, thus putting us to the test in this world. He bestowed upon us freedom to opt for either good or evil on condition that we shall be content with the result that we receive.

As a precondition of the worldly trial, He determined different life conditions for each of His servants.

Human beings are created with different abilities and conditions in order to insure the continuity of human social life in order, harmony, and peace. If all human beings were endowed with identical qualities, identical vocational capabilities, and identical material and spiritual conditions, there could be no division of labor in society, and consequently, no peaceful order of human life. Instead, human beings are created to need each other, just as our two hands need each other in order to wash themselves. The course of human life is designed for all people to cooperate in its affairs, just as all parts of a machine are necessary for the sound functioning of the machine. Thus the fact that human beings have different opportunities in this worldly realm of trial is not without wisdom.

Different circumstances create different responsibilities for the faithful, as well as allotting different rights. One's social position, whatever it may be, makes special demands upon conscience and faith. Allah the Almighty has required his poor, weak and needy servants to be patient; they will receive compensation in the Hereafter for what they suffer in this world. Allah the Almighty has also required his rich, powerful, and capable servants to beware greed and arrogance; they must be thankful instead.

Giving thanks to Allah is not a matter of words. The true way to give thanks is to offer sustenance to those who need it. It is supporting the weak for the pleasure of Allah, seeking to meet their needs and receive their blessings. Acts like these are the best expressions of gratitude.

Surely now and then we must ask ourselves, "I am strong and healthy: why is so-and-so handicapped and ill? I am wealthy: why is so-and-so poor?" We should answer these questions by reasoning, "Allah has entrusted these bounties to me, so I am responsible for them. I must do my best to use these opportunities to help those who lack them."

The Prophet ﷺ said, "Whoever remains indifferent to a fellow Muslim's sorrow is not one of us." (Hâkim, IV, 352; Haythamî, I, 87).

A responsibility of empathy linked to religious solidarity is very important. Despite our concrete separateness, Muslims are meant to consider each other as limbs of a single body, all depending on the same heart. Just as pain suffered by one limb is felt throughout the body, so the pain of any suffering Muslim is a trial of conscience for all of us.

When Ozi Castle fell to a siege and all its inhabitants were murdered, Ottoman Sultan Abdulhamid I was profoundly grieved. "O my Lord, my soldier sons and innocent people are slaughtered!" he cried. From the depth of his sorrow he lost his health, and finally became paralyzed and died: a manifestation of a deep sense of responsibility. How great was the sensitivity, flowing from faith, that took the life of a mighty sultan! If we are to obtain divine approval, then we faithful must seek to love each other, to serve each other, and to support each another with this degree of sensitivity.

We believers also need each other for good deeds and prayers. Weak and suffering believers need the good deeds of the rich and powerful, and rich and powerful believers need the blessings of the suffering and weak.

Mawlana Jalâluddîn Rûmî expresses this elegantly:

Just as beauty seeks a clear mirror, so generosity seeks the poor. As the outer beauty of a handsome person is reflected in a mirror, so the inner beauty of a giving person is revealed through others' need.

On the other hand, those who suffer various difficulties should not consider what they experience to be punishment. They need to know that such challenges are divine tests. If they are patient and thankful to Allah in every situation, they will receive compensation for whatever they suffer.

Thus with regard to the good pleasure of Allah, the thankful rich and the patient poor are equal. The only difference between them is that one group is being tried by poverty while the other group is being tried by wealth.

To show us an example of each, Allah the Almighty tells us of the prophets Solomon and Job. Although Solomon ﷺ had unlimited wealth, he never became arrogant. Worldly possessions did not occupy his heart, and he always remained thankful to Allah. This is why Allah complimented him in the Qur'an, saying "*ni`mal-`abd*" "how excellent a servant!"[25]

On the other hand Job ﷺ, who was tried by poverty and disease, was always conscious that it was Allah who had decreed those trials should fall upon him. He accepted his condition and never complained. Because of his consent to the divine decree, Prophet Job ﷺ received the same divine compliment, "*ni`mal-`abd*" "how excellent a servant!",[26] as did Prophet Solomon. Thus the important thing in the view of Allah is not how a certain servant is tried, but rather how he responds to his trial.

This is why sincere believers should above all aim to be content with Allah. In order to root this attitude firmly within ourselves, in spiritual affairs we should admire and emulate people who are more virtuous than we are. In material affairs, we should keep in mind those who are worse off , and be thankful. We should not complain about difficult conditions decreed by Allah the Almighty, but be consoled by our faith that the conditions we suffer from will lighten our accounting in the Hereafter. For Allah the Almighty will question most strenuously those to whom He gave the most resources in the life of this world. Those who received less bounty shall be held less responsible. Divine justice will then manifest in this manner.

It follows that a person born into a primitive or an ignorant society is less responsible for accepting true religious beliefs than a person born into a religious and civilized society: their conditions

25. See, Sa'd 38/30.
26. See, Sa'd 38/44.

are not comparable. Hence the divine gifts bestowed upon each servant are the factors that determine the limits and the degree of our responsibility.

In the noble Qur'an Allah says:

Allah tasks not a soul beyond its scope. (Baqarah, 2/286)

That is, Allah holds His servants responsible exactly to the extent of the power and opportunity He grants us. This implies that each of us is answerable for every undertaking we might have carried out, and yet did not. We must keep well in mind that we shall be held accountable in the Hereafter for each good deed we could have done but refrained from doing, as well as for unprovided services such as advising others toward faith and good works, and warning them against injustice and evil.

At this point, an important problem emerges for serious Muslims. For while it is easy to estimate the amount of alms that we owe on our wealth, it is difficult to identify how much service we owe due to our other worldly benefits, let alone the spiritual gifts bestowed upon us by Allah. For example, making an effort in the cause of Allah is a duty with which Allah the Almighty taxes the servant. However, unlike almsgiving, its amount or proportion is never defined.

If your wealth is so great that you properly owe a hundred million dollars in alms, your responsibility is not discharged if you pay out a million to the poor. The responsibility resulting from spiritual gifts may be considered in similar terms. Some people receive more such gifts, and others, fewer. Let's say that the heart-capacity of the latter is a little cup, while the heart-capacity of the former is a big kettle. If a person who has a big kettle pours out of it only a cup's worth of water, that means he is either miserly or pointlessly carrying around an empty kettle. Capacity is a matter of divine decree, and the differences among us makes us responsible to different degrees.

Since it is impossible to know the exact amount of responsibility due for the divine gifts given us, we should never place too much trust in the designated prayers that we have performed or the good deeds and works of charity that we have carried out. It may be that the capacity of our "responsibility container" is so large that our good deeds are very far from filling it!

We receive many illustrations of this principle from the Age of Felicity. For instance, a Bedouin once came to the Prophet ﷺ and declared that he would observe only the compulsory acts of worship. The Prophet ﷺ remarked: "If he keeps his promise, he will be delivered."[27] This was because the capacity of that person was only that much. However, the Prophet ﷺ repeatedly advised Mu'âdh, one of his close Companions, that his observances were "not enough." Finally the Prophet ﷺ said to him, "Shall I inform you of the thing on which the fulfillment of all these depends?" When Mu'âdh said: "Yes, please, O Messenger of Allah!" The Prophet ﷺ grasped his tongue and said, "Protect your tongue!"

Mu'âdh then asked: "Are we held responsible for what we say?" And the Prophet ﷺ replied, "O Mu'âdh! May Allah make you good! The thing that pushes people to Hell is only the words produced by tongues!"[28]

We have no certainty whether we hold a cup or a large kettle in our hand, that we might identify the degree of our responsibility. In fact, we don't even want to know. Perhaps we have a big barrel

---

27. For the details of this event, see Bukhârî, Imân 34; Sawm 1; Shahâdât 26; Muslim, Imân 8 and 9.
28. For the details of this event, see Tirmidhî, Imân, 8; Ibn Mâja, Fitan, 12.

of responsibilities! Still, each of likes to pretend, "I have only a little cup....so it's enough for me to give a little from my little cup!" Many people who enjoy great divine bounty and so are holding large barrels still compare themselves to those who hold small cups, and say of their few good deeds that "I have filled my cup." Many other people are totally out of their minds: they compare their private situation to the overall wealth of society, discount their vast resources, and comfort their consciences by taking care of themselves, leaving the whole work to others.

However, we must know that divine gifts bestowed upon a society and those given to individuals are not to be compared. That is why we should never feel satisfied with the services that we provide for the cause of Allah. We should never assume that we have fulfilled our duty completely. In order to meet our responsibility for the divine gifts granted us, we must keep making efforts until our last breath.

We must also be careful of falling into the trap of considering ourselves exempt from making efforts in the cause of Allah because we suffer some deprivation. Our example is Abdullah ibn Umm Maktûm ﷺ, of the Companions of the Prophet, who was blind. Nonetheless he participated in the Qadisiya military expedition, saying, "I can carry the flag, at least!" Another example comes from the Tabuk campaign. A poor Companion was regarded as exempt from participating because he did not have a mount. But he joined the expedition anyway by reaching an agreement with another Companion to borrow his mount. The agreement was that if they won the battle and he survived, he would give his entire share of the war booty in exchange for the use of the mount. The people of that time showed many such examples of self-sacrifice. They understood that the degree of effort necessary to carry out a good deed increases the reward one gets in return.

All sincere services undertaken to please Allah are signs of maturity of heart. They are all occasions to get closer to our Lord. Thus even if we suffer some disease, disability, or poverty, we should not abandon serving Islam, saying that "I have a valid excuse..." Instead, we should clear obstacles from the way and try hard to do everything we can to serve the religion of Allah.

Allah says in the noble Qur'an:

O you who believe! If you help Allah, He will help you and will make your feet firm. (Muhammad, 47/7).

Don't endanger yourselves!

During the `Umayyad period, the Muslim military, wishing to realize the prediction of the Prophet ﷺ regarding the conquest of Constantinople, the Byzantine capital, advanced very close to the city. Among the soldiers was Abû Ayyûb al-Ansârî, the famous Companion who had served as the Prophet's host in Medina when the Prophet ﷺ departed Mecca.. The fighting was intense, and the Byzantine soldiers were protected by the city's great walls. A Muslim soldier from Medina charged his horse into the Byzantine army. Seeing how dangerous the situation was and keeping in mind the divine command, "*be not cast by your own hands into ruin,*" the Muslim army was shocked. " My God!" they said, "Look at him, running blatantly into danger!"

Overhearing this, Abû Ayyûb al-Ansârî told them, "That Qur'anic verse was revealed about us, the original Muslims of Medina. After Allah made his religion prevail through the surrender of Mecca, we said: 'From now on, let's take care of our own possessions and work to make them more profitable and fruitful.' Then the verse was revealed to the Prophet ﷺ :

Spend your wealth for the cause of Allah, and be not cast by your own hands into ruin; and do good. Lo! Allah loves the beneficent. (Baqarah, 2/195).

"'Casting oneself by one's own hands to ruin' shows the danger of being occupied with private affairs and neglecting the responsibility of making efforts in the cause of Allah."

Such was the situation of Abû Ayyûb al-Ansârî. Having observed this divine warning with outmost sincerity, and being concerned with fulfilling his responsibility, he never considered his deeds enough and never stopped trying his best in the cause of Allah. During a military expedition, in which he participated with the passion of his faith, he reached the rank of martyrdom. He was eighty years old. (See Abû Dâwûd, Jihâd, 22/2512; Tirmidhî, Tafsîr, 2/2972).

Caliph 'Umar ibn 'Abd al-Azîz, whose two-and-a-half year reign was filled with great achievements, used to reflect self-critically. As his wife consoled him, he would say, "O Fâtimah! What will I say when my Lord questions me about the people under my rule? And what will I say if the Messenger of Allah reminds me of my responsibility?" When he reflected on these issues, they say, one could easily discern how he was struggling, like a bird fallen into water, fluttering its wings....

In the noble Qur'an, Allah says:

"O you who believe! Observe your duty to Allah with right observance, and die not save as those who have surrendered (unto Him)." (Âl Imrân, 3/102).

"And serve your Lord till the Inevitable (death) comes unto you." (Hijr ,15/99).

"So when you are relieved, still toil, and strive to please your Lord." (Inshirâh, 94/7-8).

Following the holy verses, we should keep making efforts with all our heart and increasing frequency until the end of our lives. Again, the Prophet ﷺ is our example in this regard. He used to pray all night until morning asking Allah for forgiveness, even though his past and future sins had all been forgiven.

When his community was building its mosque, the Prophet ﷺ carried stones on his back. He used to collect firewood to cook the family meal when they went out to the fields. When the Muslim army was on the march during the Badr campaign, he traded time on his camel in shifts with three of his Companions. Those Companions tried to waive their turns to his advantage, but he would not accept that, saying "You are not better walkers than I am, and I am not less needy of divine rewards than you are." (Ibn Sa`d, II, 21; Ahmad, I, 422)

To sum up, since we cannot measure the capacities and opportunities that Allah has bestowed upon us, we must dedicate ourselves until our last breath to serving the cause of Truth as much as we can.

❂

The best way to pay what we owe for the divine gift of faith is to explain the message of Islam to people without faith and sinners. We should guide them to Islam in a respectful and acceptable manner. One must be careful. Sinful people are like wounded birds -- they are cured not by anger, but by mercy. We must never transfer our dislike of sin to a dislike for the sinner. Such refined behavior is more easily learned in an environment influenced by a proper Sufi perspective.

Nowadays, since many people suffer from weakness of will, we must behave like doctors in a hospital. Just as providing sick people with the road to recovery is the humanitarian responsibility of a doctor, so providing guidance toward the cure for people's spiritual diseases is our responsibility.

Indeed, our Prophet ﷺ said: "Religion is advice." (Bukhârî, Imân, 42). So that we might grasp that advice should be provided repeatedly, he repeated his saying three times.

Don't trust in your deeds!

No human deed is enough to pay back our debt of gratitude to Allah for all His gifts. This is why virtuous and good servants, and even prophets, wish to be judged not merely on the basis of their deeds, but also on the basis of divine forgiveness and mercy.

One day, the Messenger of Allah ﷺ asked his Companions to keep away from extremes and to lead a balanced life. "Keep to the middle way, be straightforward (in religion). Beware! None of you can be saved simply because of his deeds."

His Companions responded with surprise, "O Messenger of Allah, does this also apply to you?"

And our Prophet ﷺ said: "It applies to me as well. However, if Allah forgives me out of his mercy and generosity, that is something else!" (Muslim, Munâfiqîn, 76, 78)

In an another Prophetic tradition it is declared: "Even if a man were to make continuous efforts and keep prostrating in worship from the day of his birth till the day of his death, his deeds would still be insufficient on the Day of Judgment." (Ahmad, c. IV, s. 185).

That is, even such a devoted and pious believer should understand that his deeds by themselves are not enough to save him.

Our Prophet ﷺ affirmed that human beings are unable to worship Allah as He deserves. He took this position even though

125

he himself used to worship so much during the night that his feet would become swollen. His prayer was, "O my Lord! I am unable to praise You as You deserve! Only You can praise Yourself!" (Muslim, Salât, 222)

Accordingly, that which is proper for us is not to console ourselves by our deeds, but to ask Allah for forgiveness and generosity, even while we are working hard.

❀

There can be no doubt that our responsibilities are heavier than ever in this time of spiritual crisis when people are ruined under the yoke of temporary delights and paltry desires. May our Lord grant that we make efforts appropriate to our responsibilities! May He forgive our faults and shortcomings and honor us all with His Paradise and His beauty.

Amin...

CHAPTER 8

Consciousness of Trusteeship

The Messenger of Allah ﷺ declared that believers have important responsibilities toward each other. He told us that the faithful should be bound together like the bricks of a wall and that all of us should feel the grief experienced by any of us. He further warned us that to sleep with a full stomach while one's neighbor is hungry is not compatible with Islamic ethics. In short, believers are entrusted to each other.

CONSCIOUSNESS OF TRUSTEESHIP

The term *al-mu'min,* which is the general term used to indicate anyone who believes in Allah, is also one of the beautiful divine names. When it is used for Allah, it indicates that Allah is the source of security. He provides confidence to the faithful and He makes them safe. It is also Allah who assigns to His messengers the attribute of faithfulness: He is the one who makes them trustworthy. Considered in this way, a "person of faith" is a person who *keeps* faith, a reliable person who inspires a sense of security in others.

A sense of respect toward that which is entrusted to them helps keep alive the bonds of faith among believers. A strong Prophetic warning states this truth:

When Allah the Mighty and Majestic wishes to ruin a servant, He removes modesty from him. Having lost modesty, that servant falls under divine wrath. Having fallen under divine wrath, he loses trustworthiness. Without trustworthiness, he can only be a betrayer. Having become a betrayer, he loses mercy. When mercy is lost, he is blameworthy and damned. When he is blameworthy and damned, his ties to Islam are cut off! (Ibn Mâja, Fitan, 27).

As the Prophetic tradition explains, trustworthiness is one of the conditions insuring soundness of faith. This is why Allah warned us on many occasions to carefully protect it. Here are some examples from the Qur'an.

And if one of you entrusts (anything) to another, let him who is trusted deliver up that which is entrusted to him (according to the pact between them) and let him observe his duty to Allah his Lord...
(Baqarah, 2/283)

...Whoso embezzled will bring what he embezzled with him on the Day of Resurrection. (Âl Imrân, 3/161)

O you who believe! Betray not Allah and His messenger, nor knowingly betray your trusts. (al-Anfâl, 8/ 27)

Lo! Allah commanded you that you restore deposits to their owners, and, if you judge among people, that you judge justly... (Nisa', 4/ 58)

Trustworthiness is one of the five distinctive properties of prophets. Even before Islam, our Prophet ﷺ was known as an extremely trustworthy person among the Arabs, who gave him the names "the Faithful" (*al-amin*) and "the Reliable" (*as-sadiq*) Even Abu Jahl, who was the archenemy of the Messenger of Allah, said to him, "O Muhammad! I'm not saying that you're a liar. But I don't accept the message you brought..." By uttering such a statement, he was confessing that he accepted the truthfulness of our Prophet ﷺ, but was defeated by his selfish desires. Indeed, this situation is stated in the following verse of the holy Qur'an:

"...though in truth they deny not you (Muhammad); the evildoers flout the revelations of Allah." (An`âm, 6/33)

For respecting trusts and keeping promises, no one came close to the Prophet ﷺ. Abdullah ibn Abil-Hamsa ﷺ related a good example.

Before he was sent as a prophet, I had a business transaction with the Messenger of Allah, and I became indebted to him. I told him that I would make payment immediately if he waited for me, and I departed from that place. But I forgot my promise. After three days, I remembered it. When I went back to the place where we had talked, I found that he was still there. Yet the Messenger of Allah did not get angry because of what I had done. He only said, "Young man, you have inconvenienced me! I have been waiting for you for three days." (Abû Dâwûd, Adab, 82/4996).

Our Prophet ﷺ was known among his people for integrity, justice, and dependability. Indeed our mother Khadîja, who was a noble and respected woman of Mecca, admired his great personality to such an extent that she proposed marriage to him.

Even those Jews of Medina who were opposed to the spread of Islam used to consult him when they got into disagreements among themselves, because they were sure of his justice and integrity. And the Messenger of Allah ﷺ would resolve their disputes.

When the letter in which the Prophet ﷺ invited the Byzantine Emperor Heraclius to Islam reached the emperor at Damascus, Abû Sufyân was also visiting that city. Heraclius asked Abû Sufyân many questions about our Prophet ﷺ. The emperor wondered whether the Prophet ﷺ was ever accused of being a liar, whether he used to keep his promises. Even though he was at that time an enemy of Islam, Abû Sufyan felt compelled to say that the Prophet ﷺ never lied and never broke his promises.

Thus we see that even those who did not believe in the prophethood of our Prophet ﷺ acknowledged his integrity and truthfulness. Indeed, when he emigrated from Mecca, he was holding some items entrusted to him by local polytheists. Our Prophet ﷺ appointed Ali to return those items to their owners.

In short, Muslims as well as non-Muslims trusted him.

His sense of truthfulness was extremely strong. Once a woman called her baby, saying. "Come! See what I'll give you!" The Prophet ﷺ asked her what she meant to give the baby. She told him she would give the child some dates. The Prophet ﷺ remarked, "If you were to give him nothing, you would be committing the sin of lying." (Abû Dâwûd, Adab 80 / 4991; Ahmad, III ,447) His sensitivity applied not only to people but also to animals. When he saw that one of his Companions called his horse by giving the false impression that he held something the horse could eat, he was so disturbed that he called the man and warned him not to deceive it. (See Bukhârî, Imân, 24)

Since our Prophet ﷺ looked at Creation with a mercy bestowed upon him by the Creator, he was careful toward all creatures. Once, while the Muslims were returning from a military expedition, a few Companions scooped some baby birds out of a nest and petted them. Then the mother bird returned. She could not find her nestlings and started fluttering her wings in pain. When the Messenger of Allah learned of this, he ordered the Companions to put the baby birds back immediately and not to harm the mother. (See, Abû Dâwûd, Jihâd, 112)

Ibn Abbâs ﷺ related that a man was sharpening his slaughtering-knife while the sheep he was going to butcher was lying before him. Allah's Messenger said, "How many times do you want to kill it? You should have sharpened your knife before having it lain before you." (Hâkim, IV, 257)

He prohibited people from breaking a green branch. He reported that a certain woman who performed religious prayers but left her cat hungry, would go to Hell for the sake of the cat, while a sinful woman who provided water for a dog about to die of thirst would receive the divine mercy. He considered all creation as entrusted to humanity by Allah, and wanted the faithful to be the representatives of security and peace on earth.

Every Muslim must be aware of the fact that he or she belongs to the community of a prophet who assumed the attributes of the Faithful (*al-Amîn*) and the Reliable (*as-Sâdiq*). Accordingly, a believer must be faithful in word and in deed. All other people, even all other creatures, must be safe from a believer's hands and tongue. A believer is meant to demonstrate strong Islamic character, because people admire exemplary persons with strong character and dignity, and so they follow them. Our Prophet ﷺ wanted his community to make trustworthiness part of its identity.

The Messenger of Allah urged believers, "Return the item that is entrusted to you (on time). Don't betray (even) those who betray you!" (Abû Dâwûd, Buyû', 79/3534) He considered losing entrusted items to be a cause of grave corruption. One day while he was conversing with his Companions, a man asked the Prophet ﷺ, "When will the Day of Judgment come?"

He replied, "Wait for the day of judgment when people spoil things that are entrusted to them."

The man persisted, "When will people spoil things that are entrusted to them?"

And the Prophet ﷺ replied, "Wait for the day of judgment when people entrust affairs to unqualified persons!" (Bukhârî, Ilm, 2)

All the divine gifts bestowed upon humanity are items held in trust. In his Farewell Sermon the Prophet ﷺ said, "…I am entrusting you with two important things. As long as you hold fast to them, you won't go astray. They are the Book of Allah and the practice of his Prophet…" Thus the Holy Qur'an and the Noble Prophetic

Tradition are the most sacred things entrusted to us by Allah and His messenger.

The Messenger of Allah ﷺ also declared that believers have important responsibilities toward each other. He told us that the faithful should be bound together like the bricks of a wall and that all of us should feel the grief experienced by any of us. He further warned us that to sleep with a full stomach while one's neighbor is hungry is not compatible with Islamic ethics. In short, believers are entrusted to each other.

Adopting the principle that one must show mercy to all creatures for the sake of their Creator, our Ottoman ancestors established more than 26,000 charitable foundations. They tried to serve humanity, animals, and even plants. That was the result of their viewing creation as a trust. In the absence of such a vision, what would have led our noble forefathers to assist the believers living in Aceh (now Indonesia), which is located at the other end of the world, with all available means? They helped those distant Muslims materially, as well as offering them military support against the colonial powers. Their sense of responsibility extended not only to their own country but also beyond.

The precious homeland in which we are brought up is also a sacred trust. Observance of religious duties, and protection of life, honor, and property, are possible only through protection of our homeland. The emigration of our Prophet ﷺ to Medina conveys much wisdom in this regard, for it indicates the importance of having a secure homeland in order to live according to one's religion.

Looking at our history, we see that the land we live in became a homeland for us through the blood of martyrs, who died for the honor of bearing the trust of Islam to the rest of the world. Conscious of protecting this trust, Alparslan wrapped himself in a white garment – that is, his shroud – and told his soldiers, "Today, we are all the same!" He inspired his soldiers by intending martyrdom himself. When Suleiman the Magnificent looked out over his victorious navy, which had turned the Mediterranean Sea into an Ottoman lake, he remarked, "Now it is not a time for boasting and pride. It is a time for thanking Allah, who has granted us this victory!" When Ottoman military units on the march foraged the countryside for provisions, they used to leave payment for the produce they took hanging on the branches of trees. This is a remarkable illustration of how the trusteeship of the homeland was understood in those days. And when Osman Pasha, the veteran of Pleven, believed he could no longer protect his non-Muslim citizens, he repaid them the tax he had collected from them. This is another striking manifestation of the consciousness of trusteeship and justice.

Allah the Almighty helps believers when they defend their country and religion. The following event is remarkable: it shows the mental state and degree of faith of our recent ancestors, and took place during the Çanakkale War (the Dardanelles campaign of World War I).

It was just one day before the festival celebrating the end of Ramadan. Vehip Pasha, the commander of the front, unenthusiastically summoned the young imam of the 9th Division. "O Imam!" he said. "Tomorrow is the Ramadan Festival. Soldiers want to do festival (eid) prayer together. Despite my best efforts, I could not change their minds. However, the situation is quite dangerous. The moment may turn out to be an opportunity for the enemy to attack and destroy us altogether. I need you to explain it to the soldiers in a manner they can understand!"

Immediately after the Imam left the Pasha's presence, a man with a shining face appeared to him.

"O my son!" the mysterious man said to the Imam. "Beware! Don't say anything to the soldiers! Let's wait and see. Things happen only according to the divine decree."

The Imam decided to listen to the old man and say nothing. Next morning, when the soldiers gathered in community for the great festival prayer, their hearts filled with divine love, a miracle occurred. Clouds descended and covered the gathering. The enemy forces who were watching them through binoculars could make out nothing but the clouds. That morning the soldiers performed the festival prayer with a new spiritual joy. Their strong voices declaring the greatness of Allah rang to the heavens. While the bright-faced old man recited some verses from the Qur'anic chapter Fath (Victory), soldiers shouted the Affirmation of Unity, the profession of faith of Islam. The sound was heard even in the enemy headquarters. Great disorder broke out among the English forces. Some Muslim soldiers from the British colonies, overhearing the praise of Allah, became aware for the first time that they were fighting against Muslims like themselves. They rebelled against their commanders. The English commanders executed some of them by shooting, and were obliged to send the rest away from the front.

This is how the trusteeship of the homeland came down to us: upon the shoulders of people whose hearts were filled with faith, who provided fit occasions for examples of divine aid. Those Ottoman soldiers who were called Mehmetciks (humble imitators of Muhammad ﷺ) were distinguished by their love of Allah and His Messenger, and dedicated themselves to be sacrificed for Truth. They did not leave aside recitation of the Qur'an, observance of formal prayer, or chanting the Beautiful Names of Allah even during the turmoil of battle. They ran from one front to another, hoping that a moment of martyrdom would be their time for meeting their

Lord. They were firmly convinced that nations who hold fast to religion, who keep going in the direction indicated by the Qur'an, and who make faith in the unity of Allah their hallmark shall live perpetually, while nations who leave the Qur'an and fall into the darkness of ignorance shall reach a terrible end. For a prophetic tradition says, "Certainly, Allah the Almighty elevates some nations because of this Book (the noble Qur'an – i.e., because of their compliance with the divine commands in it), and He abases others because of (their being away from the direction indicated by) it." (Muslim, Musâfirîn, 269)

One should look for divine self-disclosure in the fact that the Ottomans grew into a world power out of a tribe of four hundred tents through a remarkable respect for the Holy Qur'an and the institution of a military so reverent toward religion that it "erected minarets wherever it went."

One should also remember, as an example of this remarkable respect, that sacred relics of the Prophet ﷺ were brought to Istanbul during the reign of Sultan Selim; that they were preserved in a special place in Topkapi Palace allocated to them; that the Ottomans established a tradition of reciting the Qur'an at that spot that has continued for centuries; and that the one who recited the Qur'an there first was Sultan Selim himself.

We must not forget that the secret lying beneath the glory of nations in the external and internal realms is their observance of the wisdom of the spiritual realm. All the magnificence in the history of the Ottoman state, which lasted for more than six hundred years, was the result of the Ottoman emphasis on spirituality.

Thus, as Muslims, our duty to our history is to educate generations of youth who have faith, who are committed to their spiritual values, and who love their homeland. This is because the protection of faith, honor, family, life, and property is possible only through the protection of the homeland.

Just as our forefathers, passed it on to us at the cost of their lives and possessions, so we too must pass on to future generations our Muslim lands, where the Qur'an is openly recited and prayer is freely called, in better condition than we found it. In fact, Allah warns,

Then, on that day, you will be asked concerning the profit (you enjoyed in the world). (Takâthur 102/8).

The most enjoyable of divine gifts is to be free to carry out one's religious duties in one's country. One should give heed to the suffering of the Palestinians, and to the painful state of the Aqsâ Mosque, as a sad indication of what may happen when people lose their consciousness of trusteeship. The poet Mehmet Âkif told this truth to the ages:

A country without a defender is doomed to be destroyed, If you defend it, this homeland shall not be destroyed!

Even so, nations can remain alive only through cultural values that are specific to their own characters and shaped by Islam. Our sensitivity toward religion and toward history are both important trusts.

Religion is purpose in creation. It manifests as a compilation of divine laws capable of organizing the lives of individuals from cradle to grave, and preparing them for happiness in the Hereafter. Language is the means for communicating the truths established by religion. History is the torch that illuminates the future of nations through an analysis of the causes and results of events formed through language and religion. That is why culture and faith are inseparable.

We must learn our Islamic history properly, and teach it properly. It is not possible to adequately explain a universal civilization through the writings of pseudo-nationalist historians laboring under the influence of Western scholars who are enemies of Islam. Islamic history, and particularly the Age of Felicity, offers solutions to all kinds of problems. If we are well-acquainted with the life of the Prophet ﷺ, we will be always find answers for new situations.

Here is how the Prophet ﷺ treated his enemies when they were in need, and how he treated the captives of war.

In the eighth year of the Hijrah, the Meccans were suffering from a severe drought. The Prophet ﷺ sent wheat, food, dates and gold to help them, despite the fact that they had been tormenting him and his community for more than twenty years. Abu Sufyan received this generous aid and distributed it to the poverty-stricken people of the Quraysh tribe. Such aid may soften the hearts of even fierce enemies. When the gift arrived, Abu Sufyan said, "May Allah reward the son of my brother with good: he has kept his duty toward his relatives!" In this way the Prophet ﷺ softened the hearts of the Meccans toward Islam. Some of them became Muslim on that occasion, while others accepted Islam later. (Ya'qûbî, *Târîkh*, II, 56)

Another example from the life of the Prophet ﷺ relates to the battle of Badr. The Prophet ﷺ discussed with his Companions the future of the captives taken on that occasion. The decision was that wealthy captives could ransom themselves with property, while poor captives could ransom themselves by teaching reading and writing to the children of Madinah. Each poor captive was settled in a family and assigned to teach ten children; the Prophet ﷺ instructed these families to treat their lodgers very well. The brother of Mus'ab ibn 'Umayr Abû 'Azîz related his experience as such a captive:

I was a captive of war at the battle of Badr and was yielded to a family of Ansar (Madinian Muslims). The Messenger of Allah had told them to treat us very well. At that time, bread was very scarce. In order to fulfill the Prophet's instruction, this family gave their small amount of bread to me, leaving themselves with only dates to eat. I was ashamed to eat their bread while they had nothing to eat themselves. I wanted to give it back, but they insisted that I take it. (Haythamî, VI, 86; İbn Hishâm, II, 288)

If we wish to revive our glorious civilization, then we should carefully study these examples, and countless others from the history of Islam. History bears witness that nations and individuals organize their lives according to their past experience. History is the memory of nations. Nations will always need the warning and guidance of historical events. As long as a nation recognizes and pays due respect to its true history and material and spiritual leaders, it is an advanced nation and a great one. If upcoming generations come to know their own history better than foreigners do and take heed of the experience of the past, there is no ground for worry about the future! As for those who do not rely on the past, their future is never secure. Roots must go deep into yesterday if branches are to reach tomorrow.

It would be a grave mistake to take the science of history as simply an enumeration of past happenings. The true science of history is full of wisdom. It establishes the ground that separates truth from falsehood in the stories of nations, which are full of various events. In order to properly organize the future of nations, this ground must be properly known and its lessons must be carefully considered. The poet Akif said:

They define history as repeating itself.

If people took heed of it, it would repeat itself!

We need to know the history of Prophetic times. We need to know the weaknesses and strengths of other Muslim nations and states. And we need to know our own history. Our Muslim fore-fathers, the Ottomans, established a society based on faith. They protected their dignity at the cost of their lives, and they were never enslaved. Our past shows us that a lion cannot be kept in a cage. As long as our nation preserves its noble characteristics, it cannot be bound into slavery.

As for us today, if we are integrated into the national and spiri-tual values of our forefathers, we will be able carry with honor the trust that they left to us. If we watch silently while our national and spiritual values are destroyed, it means we are ignorant of the trust, and may lose it. We should make serious efforts to protect the trusts bestowed upon us at the cost of so many lives. If we do, we will not need to pay a higher price to regain those trusts tomorrow. History attests that unprotected trusts are lost, and only the deserving may get them back.

May our Lord make us and future generations successful in protecting our sacred trusts! May He protect us from falling into the swamp of ignorance through neglect of our inheritance. May He grant us the gift of reaching His presence with hearts consoled by our fulfillment of trusteeship.

Amin...

CHAPTER 9

Contemplation

When we observe the world reflectively, we discover many questions hidden in the depths of our souls. Where do we come from? Why do we exist? Why does the universe exist? What is the origin of the resources that sustain us? How should we live? What should we believe? Where are we going? What is the ultimate meaning of life? How can we work out the mystery of the reality of death? How can we make ourselves ready for death?

❈

A soul that is open to contemplation easily perceives that the direction of the body in prayer is the Ka`bah, but the direction of the soul in every moment is Allah.

CONTEMPLATION

The ability to reflect, to consider, is a vital gift with which not only humans, but all beings, are endowed. Every creature uses this gift in its own world in accordance with the pattern of its creation. Among animals, the ability to consider serves the preservation of bodily life and selfhood. Its scope is the furtherance of drinking and eating, the increase of ease, and the production of descendants. Therefore a wild animal's way of reflection focuses on hunting and mating. Apart from that, it has no thoughts or concerns: those are its limits. It never considers the nature of the universe or the future of the world. With human beings, however, the picture changes.

Sensual mind and spiritual mind

Since human beings are created as the most honorable and valuable creatures in the universe, our accountability and mission are great. We are therefore endowed with an immense ability for contemplation.

Human beings can deserve Paradise not because of our sensual mind concerned with eating and drinking, the increase of ease, and the production of descendants, but because of our spiritual mind: the honor and dignity with which we have been specially endowed.

If a human being does not actively develop the capacity for spiritual reflection, the capacity can be lost. The resulting life of heedlessness will in the end bring nothing but repentance, in old age, for a life spent on nothing but foolishness in childhood, ignorance in adolescence, and lustfulness in youth. Eating, drinking, and gathering worldly possessions easily lead to our losing our ability to contemplate in a whirlpool of sensual desires. One mystic said, "For the wise, this world is a stage for the contemplation of divine art. For the ignorant, it is a stable for the accommodation of desires."

Thus, what makes people truly human is an engagement in spiritual reflection that nurtures a climate of consciousness. Allah the Almighty wishes His servants to have faith in Him and to worship Him with profound awareness. And this is possible only by contemplating divine greatness.

Development of soul

One of the major responsibilities of the servant of Allah is to develop the soul through deep contemplation. Perfection in morality, kindness in behavior, vigilance of heart, and surrender in worship follow from contemplation that furthers a growing soul.

If we look at the beauties of creation as an object lesson, we will no doubt find illustrations of wisdom. We will notice an elephant, for example, managed by a ten-year-old child. We will see a mighty wrestler who has never been beaten by another wrestler forced down by a tiny invisible germ. So who is strong and who is weak? What are the meanings of power and powerlessness, existence and nonexistence?

When we observe the world reflectively, we discover many questions hidden in the depths of our souls. Where do we come from? Why do we exist? Why does the universe exist? What is the origin of the resources that sustain us? How should we live? What should we believe? Where are we going? What is the ultimate meaning of life? How can we work out the mystery of the reality of death? How can we make ourselves ready for death?

Such reflections, when accompanied by Qur'anic guidance and Prophetic tradition, lead the servant to an awareness of his or her own fragility and smallness. Contemplation reminds us that our sense of sovereign self-determination is a delusion. We are always in need of our Creator. Humans depend upon the Almighty Being to sustain us: all living beings must depend upon an Almighty Being. What a great mistake not be aware of this fact!

A believer who progresses toward maturity of soul through reflection harvests spirituality and wisdom in worship and service to Allah. A soul that is open to contemplation easily perceives that the direction of the body in prayer is the Ka`bah, but the direction of the soul in every moment is Allah. Hadrat Ali ﷺ observed, "Worship without knowledge, and Qur'an-reciting without contemplation, do not bring as much benefit as expected!" The value of worship performed by an ignorant soul gradually diminishes, and sometimes that worship becomes nothing but exhaustion for the worshipper.

The friends of Allah, therefore, urge us to perform each prayer as if we were performing our final prayer, to fast in consciousness of Allah's benevolence toward us, and to constantly reflect upon the poor. They recommend that we perform all of our worship as contemplation.

Abul-Darda ﷺ said, "An hour of contemplation is better than forty nights of extra prayers." (al-Daylami, II, 70-71, no: 2397, 2400). Such a condition of contemplation makes one taste all prayers more deeply, and also leads to more commitment and greater gratitude toward Allah.

As belief is fundamental in religion, so is prayer. Yet prayers are acceptable only when they are performed with a reflective heart and accompanied by spiritual vigilance. Only then will the servant come closer to Allah. The Companions of the Prophet ﷺ and the sincere believers of the subsequent generation were particularly distinguished by their contemplative hearts. Abdullah ibn Mas`ud ﷺ told his friends, "You perform more prayers than the Companions of the Prophet ﷺ did. But they were more heedless of this world, and more heedful of the next."

Our Lord wants us to contemplate His dignity and greatness, the mystery and wisdom inherent in the universe, and His benevolence toward His servants. As a result, we will understand that this life is transitory and that eternal life follows upon it. We will be good, committed, and humble servants of Allah.

Contemplation by the Prophet ﷺ

The exemplary life of the Prophet ﷺ shows us the importance of contemplation for the spiritual progress that our Lord wishes to see in His servants. The Prophet ﷺ used to pray so long at night that his feet would swell. When he closed his eyes in sleep, his heart would remain awake. Even at rest he never stopped being in contemplation and remembrance of Allah.

A'ishah, the wife of the Prophet and Mother of the Faithful ﷺ , gives us an account of how vigilant and contemplative a servant the Prophet was.

"One night the Prophet ﷺ asked me, "O A'ishah! Would you permit me to spend all night worshipping my Lord?"

I answered, "I certainly like being with you, but I like better whatever makes you happy."

So he ﷺ made ablution and started to pray. He ﷺ cried while he was praying, so much that his beard, robe, and even the floor where he prostrated became wet.

When Bilal came to call the community to morning prayer, he found the Prophet ﷺ in this condition. He asked, "O Prophet! Why are you crying? Your past and future sins have all been forgiven!"

And Prophet ﷺ told him, "Should I not be a thankful servant? I swear that tonight I was given such verses that those who do not reflect should be pitied! Then he recited:

Surely in the creation of the heavens and the earth and the alternation of the night and the day there are signs for people of understanding, those who remember Allah standing and sitting and lying on their sides and reflect on the creation of the heavens and the earth: Our Lord! You have not created this in vain! Glory be to You; save us then from the chastisement of the Fire.(Al `Imran, 3/190-191; Ibn Hibban, II, 386; al-Alusi, *al-Ruh al-Ma`ani*, IV, 157). .

The Prophet ﷺ wept all night when these verses were revealed. His tears fell like dew that a rose would envy. And the tears of the faithful who vigilantly contemplate the divine dignity and greatness in this world will be the ornament of their passing nights, and a light against the darkness of the grave.

The Prophet ﷺ practiced contemplation even before he started to receive revelation, while in seclusion in the cave on Mt. Hira. There he worshipped the Creator through contemplating the order of the heavens and the earth, as his ancestor Prophet Abraham had done.[29] And after revelation began, he persisted in that mode of

---

29. Al-`Ayni, *al-Umdah al-Qari, al-Sharh al-Sahih al-Bukhari*, Beirut, nd. I, 61; XXIV, 128.

contemplation until his death. All his speech was remembrance of Allah and all his silence was contemplation. Thus he said:

"My Lord enjoined that my silence be a form of contemplation." (I do recommend the same to you).[30]

"Contemplate the creation of Allah." (ad-Daylami, II, 56; al-Haythami, I, 81).

"There is no worship equal to contemplation." (Ali al-Muttaqi, XVI, 121).

Ahmad al-Rifa`i ☒ said: "Contemplation was the opening worship of the Prophet ☒. He had the habit of reflecting upon Allah's creation and His beneficence before every prayer. We are, therefore, meant to practice contemplation, and to make use of it to take lessons."

So let us live in an atmosphere of contemplation. Those who love the wisdom displayed in the universe are worthy of the Prophet ☒.

The vision of a blind man: an example of reflection

The Companions of the Prophet who were spiritually trained by him displayed a reflective attitude that aided them against the accidents of this world. Here is an example.

Abdullah ibn Maktum, who was a blind man, was eager to join the Muslim army before the battle of Qadisiyah. When he was told that he was exempt, he was deeply saddened. Then he reflected upon himself as a committed servant. He announced, "I can be useful even as I am. Since I cannot see the swords of the enemy, I can carry the flag in the vanguard without fear. Our soldiers will

---

30. Ibrahim Canan, Hadith Ansiklopedisi, XVI, 252, no: 5838.

follow me with courage!" The condition of this blind Companion is a striking example for those who have eyes to see....

Reading the Book of Life

Nothing in the universe has been created in vain. Every atom manifests the wisdom and goal of creation, and draws hearts to faith and love of Allah in a special way. This "speaking" of even voiceless things is called the language of state (*lisan al-hâl*). Real contemplation means to hear such language as it deserves to be heard.

Looking at events with our outward eyes alone cannot produce a mature perception of life. Observation must be accompanied by reflection. Only through mutual acts of mind and spirit can our experience of the world become an education. Only then can divine transfiguration operate to make our souls mature, powerful, and vital.

Nothing can quench our thirst for contemplation so much as comprehending and loving the Creator of the Universe. It is said in the Qur'an:

Surely it is through the remembrance of Allah that hearts are set at rest. (Ra`d, 13:28).

Our Lord sustains everything. Every occurrence in this world is bound to determined causes, and science is engaged in discovering how these causes work. However, the Causer of all causes is Allah alone. Therefore any scientific knowledge or theory that does not point to Allah, the creator of the human mind and natural law, is necessarily incomplete. It can lead to nothing but blind alleys.

Allah has commanded us, "*Read!*" We need to comprehend that command if we are ever to escape from blind alleys and useless efforts. We must adopt it as our approach to all problems and situations at all stages of our lives, since following it leads us to the source of wisdom: the primordial. Through keeping to this method, minds and hearts gain intelligence for understanding the divine will.

So let us observe all occurrences in the universe through the window of faith, and take lessons from them; let us build up our souls with contemplation. Then pearls of wisdom – insights into the divine will at the core of events – may, Allah willing, form in our hearts.

Discovering the profound: tasawwuf

The practice of tasawwuf, or Sufism, has trained many spiritual pioneers. In fact, its core is the training of the soul and the attainment of spirituality. Tasawwuf is a path that leads to the Divine Being by passing into the spiritual depths with wisdom. It is not a path that requires giving up worldly life entirely and confining oneself to seclusion. As the great poet and mystic Yunus Emre said, Sufism is not a patched cloak or a special turban; it does not mean chanting the names of Allah and nothing more.

Tasawwuf means, above all, to contemplate one's responsibilities and think over one's failures, and to make headway in comprehension of the meaning of life. It means renouncing selfishness, deepening contemplation, and moving, stage by stage, to an honorable position ending in eternal ascent.

Imam al-A`zam Abu Hanifah said, "If you want to join those Knowers, your silence should be contemplation, your looking should be lesson-taking, and your desire should be commitment to service. Those are the three features of the Knowers of Allah."

Contemplation contributes greatly to spiritual maturity in tasawwuf, since the actual objective is not to perform prayers or good deeds with an uninvolved heart, but to submit oneself to the will of the Creator in sincerity. This can only be achieved through conscious contemplation.

Contemplation of death

We can revive the heart and reach perfect spirituality only by giving up self-centeredness. Therefore the Prophet ﷺ advised, "Remember death, that destroys all pleasures." (Tirmidhi, al-Qiyamah, 26). The life of this transitory world is nothing but an instant compared to eternal life in the Hereafter. So is it wise to give preference to momentary desires?

The earth we walk on today is filled with the corpses of billions who lived before us. Their uncountable shadows overlap one another. Born into the shop of this world, they walked down an aisle filled with both selfish and spiritual needs and inclinations. After picking out either one sort or the other, they left this world through the door of death.

We will pass through the same gates. A day will come for each of us that is followed by no tomorrow. Its exact date is unknown. The declaration of our Lord is decisive:

Every soul must taste of death, then to Us you shall return. (Ankabut, 29/57).

This world is a classroom where we take lessons. It is our responsibility to be diligent and sincere students in this classroom. Let us not to be deceived by the notion that we are here in this world to stay!

153

To contemplate death is to find meaning in remembering the ultimate unknown moment before we face it. Such contemplation works by keeping us away from obsession with selfish desires; it prepares us to meet our Lord and makes us able to give a good account of ourselves in His presence. Its goal is the transformation of the face of death from an aspect of horror to an aspect of beauty. When we have overcome the lower self through contemplation of death, then we are ready to face the next world. Death is perceived as an unavoidable prelude to meeting with Allah. Then the terror of death that thrills through minds turns into anticipation. Death becomes one's wedding night, as the great Sufi Mawlana Jalaluddin said: a night of union.

So we need contemplation, perhaps more than anything else. The more we contemplate, the more success we have in educating the soul, developing strong faith, performing sincere prayers, undertaking good deeds, and awakening in ourselves a spirit that expands toward the horizon of eternal life.

May Allah help us gain mature consciousness and perception! May Allah grant us a spiritual breeze from the serene atmosphere of the Prophet ﷺ, his Companions, and the Friends of Allah! May Allah help us find peace in noble thoughts and feelings, and keep us away from the evils of selfishness! May Allah help us to apply His order" *Read!*" by examining all the incidents of life in the light of faith!

Amin…

CHAPTER 10

Rays of Wisdom From the Precincts of the Heart of Rumi

The Friends of Allah do not truly pass away even when their bodies are buried, for the hearts of perfect Muslims do not perish in the grave. Instead, their spiritual services to humanity become eternal. Many Friends of Allah who continue their service in the other world still live among us and guide us through their books and charitable foundations. They will maintain this service of leading people to the right path even after we die.

RAYS OF WISDOM FROM THE PRECINCTS OF THE HEART OF RUMİ

The Friends of Allah are the heirs of the Prophet ﷺ who put their faith into practice with love. They are the fortunate ones who illuminated their hearts through the Qur'an and the tradition of the Prophet ﷺ. For those who had no chance to meet the Prophet ﷺ and his Companions, they can serve as guides.

The Friends of Allah do not truly pass away even when their bodies are buried, for the hearts of perfect Muslims do not perish in the grave. Instead, their spiritual services to humanity become eternal. Many Friends of Allah who continue their service in the other world still live among us and guide us through their books and charitable foundations. They will maintain this service of leading people to the right path even after we die.

The relevance of their guidance passes beyond time and space. Their wise writings are like letters sent to the future with no specific address. Those letters reach everywhere, and may be read centuries after they were written.

UNESCO dedicated 2007 as the Year of Hadrat Mawlana Jalaluddin Rumi, for that is when his 800th birthday fell in the common calendar. The *Mathnawi* of Hadrat Mawlana is today among the most popular books on human spirituality in North America. This means that a sincere letter of guidance written by a Friend of Allah centuries ago still finds its reflection throughout the world long after the author's death. The work holds a mirror to the inner world of human beings, helping them know themselves better and assisting them in the solution of spiritual problems. It leads people who suffer from the materialistic mentality of this era toward spiritual tranquility.

Allah Almighty endowed the Friends of Allah with transformative capacities. They therefore act as torches of guidance, leading others with love and respect, teaching them to take Allah into their hearts.

Some Friends of Allah have been so awestruck by the grandeur of Allah that they could live only in seclusion, spending their transitory life in spiritual silence. Ibn `Abbas says of such persons, "There are certain servants of Allah who might speak with great eloquence, but their reverence toward Allah keeps them silent."

Other Friends of Allah prefer to speak but little. They are instructed by Allah to guide the wise solely through the language of actions. The following couplet by Baha'uddin al-Naqshbandi, who was one of these, alludes to that state:

The universe is wheat and I am straw.

Everyone is perfect; I am imperfect.

The most distinguished works of Baha'uddin al-Naqshbandi were the people whom he trained in his circle of conversation. Such people learned to read the lines written in his heart and conveyed them onward to other hearts through other conversations. This spiritual transmission continues even today. The teaching strategy of Baha'uddin al-Naqshbandi ﷺ was based on an instruction by

Abu Bakr 🌸, from whom he benefited greatly: "Think twice about what you speak, when you speak, and to whom you speak."

There are yet other Friends whom Allah Almighty allowed to become spiritual nightingales: they are always singing the hymns of divine love. And He made further Friends of Allah into sources whose acts and tongues are equally transmitters of wisdom.

Hadrat Mawlana in particular was given the mission of expressing divine realities in words as well as in acts. Through his words, his writings, and his actions of the heart, he has been able through the centuries to enlighten those who seek Allah and draw them closer to Him

Hadrat Mawlana was chosen as a locus of divine speech, and so has become the spokesman of the Friends of Allah. He was permitted to capture in words some of the knowledge, mystery and wisdom with which Allah Almighty had endowed him. Yet such permission is granted only up to a limit: one can express divine realities only to the extent allowed. Hadrat Mawlana may well have known far more than he wrote.

Hadrat Mawlana's own source of knowledge was undoubtedly the Qur'an and the tradition of the Prophet 🌸. He declares this in a quatrain:

I am a slave of the Qur'an as long as I live.

I am the dust of the road where Muhammad walks.

If anyone conveys a message from me denying this path of mine,

I will be grieved, perhaps disgusted, by those lies.

Mawlana Jalaluddin here clearly introduces himself as the servant of the Qur'an and the dust of the glorious path of the Prophet 🌸.

Because of this, he is both a learned scholar, drawing inspiration and illumination from the Qur'an and the Sunnah, and also a source of wisdom, interpreting divine mysteries and leading hearts toward Allah.

The Prophet ﷺ related that Hadrat Luqman advised his son, "O my son! Keep company with learned people and stay close to them! Take heed of the words of the wise! Allah Almighty revives hearts with the glory of wisdom as He revives the soil with rain." (al-Haythami, I, 125). Here are some reviving examples of Hadrat Mawlana's wisdom.

Patience and endurance

It is said in the Qur'an:

The servants of the All-Compassionate are those who walk upon the earth in humility, and when the ignorant address them, they say, "Peace." (Furqan, 25/63).

Inspired by this verse, Hadrat Mawlana said:

- "Keep quiet as a book in the company of a fool."

- "When crows scream, nightingales fall silent."

- "Know that good manners means patience with the misbehavior of the ill-mannered."

It is a very important principle in this world of trial and suffering that bearing worldly pains makes the heart mature. A persevering character is an ideal of faith. Hadrat Mawlana said:

- "My mind asked my heart, 'What is religion?' And my heart whispered in my mind's ear, 'Religion is nothing but good manners!'"

The great exemplar of good manners is the Prophet ﷺ. The Companions narrated that the Prophet's sensibilities were more delicate than a virgin girl's.

- "The rose smells sweet putting up with the thorn, for the thorn is the friend of the rose."

The universe is adorned with thousands of unspoken lessons. Here, the rose becomes the king of flowers because it shows patience toward the thorn. Happiness comes after putting up with sufferings. The door of joy opens only after we bear the failure of our earthly desires and the difficult trials of life.

Their difficult trials, misfortunes, and desperation can cause some servants to turn to their Lord, for they pray, "O my Lord, help me!" Other servants, wealthy and fortunate, may go astray and not remember their Lord at all. The egos of people who never taste despair may turn into rampaging horses beyond all human control.

The spiritual maturity of human beings grows out of the barriers we surpass. Worldly troubles and sufferings are the most important means of making spiritual progress. Allah Almighty made His messengers subject to the greatest of sufferings. Thus, all humans are subject to trial to see how conscious they are of the blessings of Allah. Allah Almighty examines all His servants in this world and will call us to account in the Hereafter.

Hadrat Mawlana advised seekers of spiritual happiness to understand the balance of life.

- "Do not sell mirrors in the market of the blind, nor sing songs in the market of the deaf."

The distinctive character of a developed Muslim is foresight and discernment. Such persons can easily grasp the mood of those with whom they converse, and then speak accordingly. Hadrat Ali says in this regard, "Speak to people according to their perceptions." (al-Bukhari, al-`Ilm, 49). This means that you should speak to people in a way that suits their understanding, not your understanding. The following principle from Rumi is very helpful for grasping the level of the perception:

- "One can discern a man's moral level from his manner of laughing, and his intellect from what he laughs at."

Seeking means come close to Allah

It is said in the Qur'an:

O you who believe! be careful of (your duty to) Allah and be with the true ones. (Tawbah, 9/119).

O you who believe! be careful of (your duty to) Allah and seek means of nearness to Him and strive hard in His way that you may be successful. (Ma'idah, 5/35).

With the message of the Qur'an Imprinted on his heart, Mawlana Jalaluddin said::

- "One is judged according to what one searches for."

- "Looking for something where it does not exist is the same as not looking for it at all."

- "Do not move before your guide moves. One who moves without a head is bound to be a tail."

- "It is better to be a slave to a Friend of Allah than to be a crown on the head of king."

Sulaiman the Magnificent, the great sultan of the Ottomans, was once welcomed by applause on the way back home from a battle that ended in victory. The Sultan was afraid of his own pride, and therefore he recited the following couplet on the necessity of training one's ego:

Being sultan of the world is nothing but stupid struggle.

Serving a friend of Allah is a greater glory!

Hadrat Mawlana says:

- "The fabric of wisdom that the soul has lost may be found in the hands of the people of heart."

- "If you unite with a man of heart, you will become a pearl even if you are as hard as stone."

- "Birds of a feather flock together."

- "One who wants to reach Allah must unite with the circle of the Friends of Allah. If you disconnect from them you are bound to perish."

- "Make friends with the Friends of Allah, so that the members of their caravan may multiply. The stronger the caravan, the less the risk of highwaymen."

It is narrated that the word *insân*, which means "human being" in Arabic, derives from the word *uns,* which means "intimacy." This shows that the human being has a native inclination to associate and make friends. One should therefore follow the divine commandment and use this human attribute to associate with the upright and the faithful believers. For every human being is under fire from the Devil and the lower self. Imam Shafi`i puts it succinctly: "If you are not occupied with what is right, you will be occupied with what is wrong."

So in order to protect oneself as an honored servant of Allah, a sincere Muslim should keep company with other committed Muslims from whom he or she can spiritually benefit. Every human being needs a spiritual guide. It is because of this need that Allah Almighty made the very first human a prophet.

Sa`di al-Shirazi makes a point about the effect of our companions on our condition. He said, "The dog of the Seven Sleepers attained great honor, gaining mention in history and in the Qur'an, for it kept company with the righteous. The wives of Prophets Noah and Lut, on the other hand, were ranked among blasphemers, for they kept company with the faithless." As this story makes clear, keeping company with ignorant and blasphemous people draws one come closer to their way of life and thought. Mental connection leads to spiritual connection, and the wrong spiritual connection can lead to spiritual corruption.

Purification of the self

It is said in the Qur'an:

He indeed shall be successful who purifies himself, and magnifies the name of his Lord and prays. (A`la, 87/14-15).

By the self and Him who balanced it, then inspired it to understand what is right and wrong for it: he will indeed succeed who purifies it, and he will indeed fail who corrupts it. (Shams, 91/7-10).

Inspired with the wisdom of these verses, Hadrat Mawlana said:

• "O traveler on the spiritual path! If you wish to know the reality, neither Moses nor Pharaoh died. Today they live within you; they are hidden in your existence. They do their fighting within you! So you had better look for those two, who are at enmity with one another, within you."

- "The human being is like a forest. Just as a forest accommodates thousands of pigs, wolves, and other animals with good and bad natures, so within us live both virtues and vices."

- "Do not seek to feed your body overmuch, for it will perish one day. It is better to nurture your soul, for that is what will reach the heavens and honor."

- "Nourish your soul with mature thinking and discernment that will give it strength for its journey."

- "When you get rid of your lower self, when you fully commit yourself to Allah, you will travel safely in the sea of divine mysteries."

- "No mirror has ever turned into iron again. No bread has ever turned into wheat again. No grape juice has ever turned into grapes again. No ripe fruit has ever become unripe again. So become mature, and prevent yourself from ever being immature again!"

- "Set fire to your lower self, dark as night, if you want to shine like the day."

Allah Almighty endowed us with life for one time only. We will not be given it again. We should, therefore, use this chance carefully to come close to Allah by reaching spiritual maturity. It is only people who develop mature personalities who do not lose much in this life. Those who yield to raw ego are bound to lose much both in this world and in the hereafter. A self which is not restrained through spiritual training and purification is like a wild horse. A wild horse leads its rider over cliffs and, therefore, to extinction, instead of taking him to his destination. Yet if a horse is trained well, it will carry its rider to her destination no matter how dangerous the journey.

Ambition, cancer of the heart

Allah Almighty states in the holy Qur'an:

...And (as for) those who hoard up gold and silver and do not spend it in Allah's way, announce to them a painful chastisement on the day when it shall be heated in the fire of Hell, then their foreheads and their sides and their backs shall be branded with it. This is what you hoarded up for yourselves, therefore taste what you hoarded. (Tawbah, 9/34-35).

Inspired by this verse, Hadrat Mawlana said:

- "No matter how rich you are, you cannot eat more than your stomach can hold. Even if you dip your water-pot into the sea, it will carry no more water than it can hold."

- "There are so many fishes which, because of ambition, swallow the bait, though the sea could safely feed them."

- "What is this world about? This world is about being ignorant of Allah!"

- "This world, a testing ground, is like a magnet for selfish desires: it attracts them as amber attracts straw. Only the substantial wheat, the wise believer whose inner world contains spiritual secrets and wisdom, can escape the attraction of this magnet."

- "The trap of raw egos is worldly gain. It tricks and allures, and the inner eyes of some people go blind out of desire for it. They drink bitter and salty water out of wet clay.

Since they never taste spiritual happiness, they regard what they taste of the worldly life as happiness."

- "Greed and ambition for the pleasures of this world lead us to obtain what we do not deserve."

Worldly ambition is the prime drive leading to great ignorance. Ambition makes the heart go blind. Such a heart ceases to draw a line between right and wrong, legitimate and illegitimate. Hadrat Mawlana says of heart-blindness, "Even a dog will not eat a bone before sniffing it." So whoever is heart-blind due to ambition for worldly attractions has less wisdom than a dog. Worldly ambition brings spiritual disaster!

Our master, Prophet Muhammad ﷺ, warned of ambition as a human failing. He said, "The son of Adam may have two valleys full of gold: he will still want a third valley. The son of Adam will be satisfied with nothing but the soil of the grave." (Bukhari, al-Riqaq, 10; Muslim, al-Zakat, 116).

Even if those afflicted with ambition attained all the wealth on earth, they would still wish to get more from the Moon or Mars. Today, the ambition and spiritual rottenness of the followers of materialism seems endless. Such is the sad condition of our world..

Abu Dharr, a Companion of the Prophet, eloquently expressed how the faithful should view property. He said, "There are three shareholders in any worldly possession. The first is its owner, which is you. The second is fate. Fate does not consult you about whether your possession will bring you good or evil, disaster or death. The third shareholder in any possession is its heir, who wants you to die. Your heir will take your property when you die, but it is you who will be held accountable for it. If you can, try not to be weakest of the three (by giving charity before death). Allah Almighty says, *"You cannot reach perfection in spending for the sake of Allah unless you give of what you love.*" My most valuable possession my camel; therefore I am giving it as a charity. I am sending it in advance so that it will welcome me in the Hereafter." (Abu Nu`aym, *al-Hilyah*, I, 163).

Worldly possessions are only entrusted to us by Allah. We do not know when what He has deposited will be withdrawn. We may lose our possessions at any time. Life is open to surprises, and we cannot tell what fate will bring. The most inescapable surprise, death, is undoubtedly on the agenda of fate. We may be ready for it always by managing the trusts we administer in the most useful of ways.

Charity, the healer of hearts and the joy of both worlds

It is said in the Qur'an:

And spend out of what We have given you before death comes to any of you, so that he should say: My Lord! why did You not respite me to a near term, so that I should have given alms and been among the doers of good deeds? (Munafiqun, 63/10).

Inspired by this verse, Hadrat Mawlana said:

• "Unfortunate souls are like dwellers in a house full of smoke. Give ear to their cries and respond by opening a window for ventilation. That will refine your soul!"

• "What have you got? What have you treasured up? What kind of pearl did you draw from the bottom of the sea? All this will be clear on the day of your death."

• "Visiting friends without a present is like going to the mill without wheat."

- "One should pay back what one owes before death takes it by force."

The following couplet by Necip Fazil puts this point eloquently:

O stingy jeweler, get another purse!

Save up a currency valid in the grave...

Wise advice is fundamental to the revival of hearts. Those who appreciate the treasures of wisdom become wise themselves. Those who follow wisdom rightly will surely perfect faith.

May our Lord give us the opportunity to live in an atmosphere of wisdom and to perceive the mysteries of reality. May He help us to comprehend the meaning of the Qur'an, of the universe, and of being human.

Amin...

CHAPTER 11

The Holy Month of Ramadan:
Spiritual Training for Life

Islam is not a religion of ceremonies practised only in the month of Ramadan or other holy times. It is a religion for all moments of life.

Ramadan is a school of commitment; the festival that follows it is its spiritual diploma. On the festival day, the faithful enjoy having passed the great examination of Ramadan. They have a brief taste of union with their Lord in this world. They will rejoice again on the Day of Judgment.

Our Lord's contentment with us is the true festival. We can claim our share of divine mercy and benevolence if we make the poor and needy happy on festival days.

CHAPTER 11

THE HOLY MONTH OF RAMADAN:
Spiritual Training For Life

Our Lord endowed the calendar of life with certain periods of spiritual gain. During those times, benevolence, forgiveness, and mercy increase. The most fruitful of such periods is the holy month of Ramadan.

- The Holy Qur'an, which is a guide for the mindful, was revealed in this month.

- The obligatory worship of fasting, which nurtures spiritual maturity, is performed in this month.

- The Night of Power, specified in the Qur'an as *better than a thousand months*, is commemorated in this month.

- The nights of this month are blessed with fast-breaking, with special prayers, and with special meals.

- The stricken hearts of the needy and deprived rejoice most in this month, because religious obligations of charity are performed in Ramadan. Obligatory or non-obligatory gifts made in this month console the poor the most.

- The doors of heaven are opened in this month.

- The doors of hell are closed because of refraining from sin.

- The devils are bound by the chains of mindfulness of Allah, *taqwa*, which is the commitment of conscious Muslims.

So the month of Ramadan not only opens up doors of eternal happiness for individual believers, but also for the whole of the Muslim world.

Qur'an and Ramadan

Allah the Almighty says:

The month of Ramadan is that in which the Qur'an was revealed, a guidance to humanity and clear proofs of the guidance, and the criterion; therefore whoever of you is present in the month shall fast in it... (Baqarah, 2/185).

It is clear from this verse that the Qur'an was revealed in Ramadan, that it is a guide for the mindful, that it presents clear proofs of the guidance for distinguishing between good and evil, and that it is incumbent on believers to fast in this month.

Thus, believers should note very well the close relation between the Qur'an and Ramadan.

Abdullah ibn `Abbas ﷺ related, "The Prophet ﷺ was the most generous among us, and he was the most generous of all when he met the Angel Gabriel in Ramadan. Gabriel, aside from bringing revelation, used to visit the Prophet ﷺ every night in Ramadan; they would recite the Qur'an together. He was even more generous than the wind of mercy [that brings rain]" (Bukhari, al-Ba`d ul-Wahy 5, 6; Sawm 7; Muslim, al-Fada'il, 48, 50).

We should properly observe the spiritual instruction given in the above narration and particularly occupy ourselves with the

Noble Qur'an during Ramadan, so that we might benefit from the blessings of the time.

In fact, every day we should set aside time for the reading of the Qur'an, which is meant to orient our daily life. But we should read more during this month. We should be occupied with the Qur'an's spiritual atmosphere, act according to its instructions, and make amends for our shortcomings.

A sound personality and a sane society can be established only through following the spiritual guidance of the Qur'an. It is a divine light enlightening the inner and outer world of believers. It is guidance for happiness, bringing us closer to Allah through its wisdom and the exemplary stories of the prophets.

The guiding power of the Qur'an can bring peace and tranquility to people who are depressed by the uncertainties of the present and the worries of the future, as well as by the complicated philosophies of modern times. Only the breadth of the Qur'an can console those depressed and confused ones, opening the ups and downs of their daily life onto a vista of eternal peace and happiness.

Ramadan as a life opportunity

Allah the Almighty swears by time in the Qur'an. He reminds us that our worldly existence lasts but an instant, and will end before the commencement of real life in the Hereafter. He thereby reminds us not to waste time. Consequently a Muslim should appreciate the blessing of time and use it efficiently for sublime goals. We should perceive the necessity of spending our lives on doing good deeds. We should hasten to worship, and ask Allah for forgiveness well before approaching the end of life.

As the whole of life is limited to certain days, so also is Ramadan. Its days, too, are numbered. So it is wise to make use of the distinctive spiritual atmosphere of Ramadan during those few days, to collect all the eternal bliss we can.

Hadrat A'ishah related: "The Prophet used to make extra effort in worship in Ramadan, to an extent we did not observe in other months. He would commit himself to even deeper worship in the last ten days of the month. He would spend whole nights praying. and would wake his family up to pray." (Bukhari, al-Fadl al-Laylat al-Qadr, 5; Muslim, al-Itiqaf, 8).

Those who make the most of Ramadan are endowed with many blessings. Those who are careless of Ramadan face great deprivation. The Prophet warned, "Angel Gabriel came to me saying: 'May the blessing of Allah avoids the one who avoids the opportunity for forgiveness in Ramadan!' And I replied saying 'Amin'..." (Hakim, IV, 170/7256; Tirmidhi, Da`awat, 100/3545).

Hold tight to fasting

Fasting is the prime concern for Muslims who wish to fulfill Ramadan. Fasting reminds us that we are, as humans, travelers heading for the Hereafter, who will be left with no earthly possession or enjoyment at the end of the journey.

Giving up worldly pleasures and thereby training one's lower self in the light of the spirit of the Qur'an is nothing but good news regarding the pleasures of heaven.

Abu `Umamah, a Companion to the Prophet, came to the Prophet one day saying, "O Prophet! Please tell me about a kind of worship for which Allah will reward me."

The Prophet ﷺ answered: "Embrace fasting! It is an unequalled worship." (Nasai, al-Siyam 43).

The Prophet ﷺ also spoke of the virtues of the pre-dawn meal: "Observe the pre-dawn meal, even if only by drinking a sip of water" (Abd al-Razzaq, *al-Musannaf*, IV, 227/7599); and "Observe the pre-dawn meal, as it contains blessing." (Bukhari, as-Sawm, 20).

Fasting in Ramadan trains us to exercise even our legitimate rights minimally As a holy month, it reminds us how careful we should be about refraining from illegitimate and dubious acts.

Abdullah Ibn `Omar ﷺ said, "Allah does not accept your worship unless you refrain from illegitimate and dubious acts, even if you pray until you grow bent as a bow and fast until you grow thin as a nail."

Hadrat Mawlana says about this point of spiritual training in fasting: "Fasting declares: 'O Allah! This person does not eat even lawful food nor drink even lawful drink, following your command-ment. How should he then extend his hands to violate your com-mandments?'"

Fasting is a spiritual discipline for controlling the raw ego. It also paves the way for improving our innate feelings of compassion and mercy.

True fasting provides us with a condition of consciousness that makes us aware of blessings and thankful for them. It leads us to sympathize with the underprivileged and to value compassion and mercy over all worldly emotions. It is a school of training that decreases greed and increases patience.

The most important lessons in our training are, of course, the tests we face in daily life. The more easily we pass such exams, the more we approach the true goal of fasting.

One of the examinations in patience we are supposed to pass during fasting is transmitted in a saying of the Prophet ﷺ : "Let none of you say bad words or quarrel while fasting. If someone swears at you or tries to quarrel with you, say, 'I am fasting'". (Bukhari, as-Sawm, 9).

Quarrelling with people is not a praiseworthy act. If a fasting person quarrels, it takes away the spiritual benefit of fasting. Allah the Almighty specifies how we should act when provoked:

And the servants of the All-Compassionate are those who walk on the earth in humility, and when the ignorant address them, they say, "Peace."(Furqan, 25/63).

So fasting should be performed in a peaceful, spiritual, and sensitive way. One should refrain from indecent and even unnecessary acts. One cannot fast properly by merely giving up eating and drinking. An acceptable fasting is performed by restraining the lower self; the lower self is restrained by keeping all parts of one's body away from illicit and dubious acts.

'Ubayd, the freed slave of the Prophet ﷺ, related, "Two women were fasting. Someone came to the Prophet ﷺ at noon to report, 'O Prophet! There are two women who are fasting and are almost dead of thirst. (Please ask them to stop fasting).'

The Prophet ﷺ turned his face away and did not answer. The one who made the request repeated his words. 'O Messenger! They are about to die!'

"This time the Prophet ﷺ answered, 'Ask them to come here!' When the two women arrived, the Prophet ﷺ gave one of them a bowl, and said, 'You had better vomit!' The woman vomited up blood, meat, and pus to the extent of half a bowl. Then the other woman did the same.

"The Prophet ﷺ said, 'These women fasted by abstaining from legitimate acts, but then broke their fast by committing illegitimate acts. They sat together and indulged in malicious talk [eating human flesh].'" (Ahmad, V, 431, al-Haythami, III, 171).

So we should not only refrain from eating and drinking, but also watch our speech. Our tongues should not be thorns stabbing at hearts, but transmitters of mercy. We need soft hearts adorned with the wisdom of the Qur'an and smiling faces reflecting the smiling face of Islam.

Being a sincere servant

The spiritual training of Ramadan is also intended to make us better servants. Those who cannot be sincere servants to Allah are bound, in the end, to become servants to other creatures. Such a condition does not befit the honor of being human. Muhammad Iqbal speaks of the misery of those who move away from Allah to become slaves to other people: "I have not seen even a dog bowing down to another dog."

So we need full consciousness of being sincere servants of Allah alone in order to have full spiritual satisfaction in Ramadan. We should therefore, improve the level of our spirituality in the month of spiritual benevolence.

The only acceptable value in this regard is sincerity. Our prayers are made most valuable by our pure hearts, good intentions, and sincerity. Any prayer devoted to egoistic aims and goals other than Allah's acceptance receive no answer. Thus, the Prophet ﷺ says, "There are many who fast and only stay hungry: they get no spiritual benefit. There are many who pray at night but only lose sleep: they get no spiritual benefit." (Ibn Maja, as-Siyam 21).

Any act that that does not lead to Allah's acceptance and does not bring profit in the Hereafter endangers one's eternal life. Making no provision for the eternal life leads to disappointment. Any prayer that is not performed in sincerity and commitment only guarantees that one will be empty-handed in the Hereafter.

Prayers performed in Ramadan should not be done in a habitual or merely traditional way, but undertaken so as to seek Allah's acceptance in sincerity. Otherwise prayers cannot bring spiritual benefit, and fasting cannot transcend being a sort of diet, and late night vigils cannot go beyond being a kind of digestive exercise.

In the great days and nights of Ramadan we should be more vigilant in our prayers. We should perform our daily prayers as if we were talking with Allah. Our prayers should become an opportunity for us to confess our failures and shortcomings and to present all our needs, both worldly and spiritual, before Allah the Almighty. Then they will be true prayers.

The Prophet ﷺ recommends that we pray in congregation. Coming together increases the value of prayer, because the congregation offers each believer spiritual depth in understanding. In every prayer we repeat the supplication,

It is You we serve and it is You we ask for help (Fatihah, 1/4).

The words inspire believers with the spirit of congregation, since the pronoun "we" indicates a group of people doing the same thing.

Prayer of supplication, or *du`a,* is the nucleus of all prayers because it allows the servant to take refuge in the Lord. It establishes our spiritual connection with Allah. Whoever breaks that connection loses his or her position in the presence of Allah. It is said in the Qur'an:

Say: My Lord would not care for you were it not for your prayer... (Furqan, 25/77).

Waking up in the middle of the night for the pre-dawn meal is also a time for spiritual training, when we benefit from the blessing of the earliest hours. At such times Allah the Almighty invites us into His presence. Believers should welcome such an invitation, and thank Allah for it. The Qur'an praises:

...the patient, and the truthful, and the obedient, and those who spend (in charity), and those who ask forgiveness in the early morning. (Al `Imran, 3/17).

The Friends of Allah regard the pre-dawn hour as a treasure. Muhammad Iqbal remarked in this regard, "I found a way of passing beyond the dome of the planet. I saw that at the pre-dawn hour, human supplications travel with greater speed than the mind can reach toward Allah, to union with Him."

To vigilantly engage in prayer before dawn lets one travel to the horizons of wisdom. Hadrat Mawlana said, "Wake up at night and walk to the Lord! Night takes you to the land of guidance. The secrets of divine love and the spiritual pleasures pour into your heart while others sleep. The windows of the heart open widest at night: then you can take you share from the worlds of spirit. Yet such events are hidden from the eyes of strangers!"

In the holy month of Ramadan, let us remember Allah and purify ourselves spiritually with every breath we take. Let us make good use of a month whose first third promises mercy, whose middle third promises forgiveness, and whose final third promises salvation. As far as we can, let us meet that generous offer with sincerity. Prayers in such a season of benefits are no doubt the most useful supplies we can lay up for our journey to the Hereafter, for the Prophet ﷺ says that our worship will accompany us in the grave. "When a believer dies he will find his daily prayers beside his head, his almsgiving on his right, and his fasting on his left." (Haythami, III, 51).

'Umar ibn 'Abdul-'Aziz said, "Make your preparations in this world based on what sort of journey you want in the grave and the Hereafter!"

The Night of Power

The Night of Power, or Destiny, is one of the treasures given to the Prophet Muhammad ﷺ as a special spiritual gift for his community. The good news of the grandeur and value of this night is announced in a Qur'anic chapter named after it, and in many sayings of the Prophet ﷺ. Here is what our Lord says about the glory of the night in Surah Qadr:

Surely We sent it down on the Night of Power. So what will make you comprehend the Night of Power? The Night of Power is better than a thousand months. The angels and the Spirit descend in it, by the permission of their Lord, upon every affair. Peace! So it is until the break of day (Qadr, 97/1-5).

The Night of Power is said to be glorified not only because the Qur'an was revealed in it, but also because a countless number of angels including the Archangel Gabriel (sometimes referred to as "the Spirit") descend in it as well. It is better than a thousand months because it is a night of blessing and benevolence in which repentant worshippers are greeted by unseen angels and forgiven by Allah.

Since it is a privileged and special night, the Prophet ﷺ sought for it among the nights of Ramadan, and asked his community to do the same. Its exact time is not specified. According to a saying of the Prophet ﷺ, it should be looked for during the eves of the odd-numbered days during the last third of the month, and on the eve of the 27th of Ramadan in particular. Yet this does not guarantee that the Night of Power will definitely fall among those days. Imam al-A`zam Abu Hanifah and ash-Shaykh al-Akbar Ibn `Arabi both argued that the Night of Power is not necessarily found in the month of Ramadan only, but might occur on any night of the year.

Imam Sha`rani's comment on the matter is very important: "For me, the Night of Power changes from year to year. I have witnessed it at various times in Sha`ban, Rabi`, and Ramadan, but I have witnessed it most often in Ramadan, and in the last days of Ramadan in particular."[31]

There is a reason why the date of the Night of Power, which is worth more than eighty-three years (one thousand months) of ordinary human life, is not specified. There is wisdom behind it. Because it is hidden, the Friends of Allah advise that one should watch for it throughout the year. Ibn Mas`ud said, "Whoever spends the whole year in vigilance is bound to discover the Night of Power." Thus the following advice has become proverbial for the faithful: "Any night could be the Night of Power; any person could be the Hidden Guide (Khidr, the guide of Moses عليه السلام in the Qur'an)."

Eid: The Festival

Days and nights of religious festivals are full of divine blessings that only committed and sensitive hearts can perceive. The Prophet ﷺ said, "Some spend the nights of the two Festivals (Fastbreak and

---

31. `Abd al-Wahhab al-Sha`rani, *al-Kibrit al-Ahmar*, p. 98, Izmir Ilahiyat Vakfi, 2006.

Sacrifice), praying for reward from Allah Alone. Their hearts will not die on the day when all hearts must die." (Ibn Maja, as-Siyam, 68).

Ramadan is a school of commitment; the festival that follows it is its spiritual diploma. On the festival day, the faithful enjoy having passed the great examination of Ramadan. They have a brief taste of union with their Lord in this world. They will rejoice again on the Day of Judgment.

Our Lord's contentment with us is the true festival. We can claim our share of divine mercy and benevolence if we make the poor and needy happy on festival days. The Prophet ﷺ says in this regard: "Show mercy to those on earth so that those in the heavens may show mercy to you." (Abu Dawud, al-Adab, 58).

It is good to keep in mind that festival days are neither days of individual celebration nor days of rest. As one cannot perform festival prayers individually, so one cannot celebrate the Festival alone or merely among one's closest family. These days are days to visit parents, relatives, and one's place of birth, and also to remember ancestors. They exist to make community stronger.

Islam is not a religion of ceremonies practised only in the month of Ramadan or other holy times. It is a religion for all moments of life.

Imam Sha`rani says, "Ramadan is given more holiness than any other month. And Allah the Almighty placed Ramadan among the months of the year so that the blessing of Ramadan could spread throughout the whole year.[32]

As Allah the Almighty gave the month of Ramadan to the whole year, so we should let the blessing and discipline we gain in Ramadan spread into the rest of our lives. And we should always

32. Abd al-Wahhab al-Sha`rani, *al-Kibrit al-Ahmar*, s. 110.

remember the spiritual pleasures we taste in Ramadan, because no matter how long we live, our life is shorter than the month of Ramadan compared to our eternity in the Hereafter.

May Allah accept our prayers for the sake of Ramadan, the blessed month! May Allah help us to live in the atmosphere of Ramadan all the time. May the months of the year form a chain from one Ramadan to the next, binding us together with sincerity and commitment. And finally, may Allah make Ramadan an agent to bring peace and happiness to our country, our nation, and all Muslims throughout the world.

Amin...

CHAPTER 13

Wastefulness - 1
Concerning Faith, Creed, and Worship

Profligacy is a word normally applied to issues of the management of wealth, but it has a wider application that includes all kinds of affairs in which human beings may exceed rightful limits. Accordingly, if a servant exceeds the limits imposed by Allah in whatever department of life, his act constitutes profligacy. All sorts of divine gifts may be spent with no profit, but only loss.

CHAPTER 13

WASTEFULNESS –1
Concerning Faith, Creed, and Worship

All the gifts bestowed by our Lord upon His servants are evidences of His mercy, compassion and love. These divine offerings are sent by Allah the Almighty to his servants freely: no servant pays anything for them or can undertake any effort in order to deserve them. Allah the Exalted declares in the holy Qur'an:

And He has made of service unto you whatsoever is in the heavens and whatsoever is in the earth (as a pure kindness). … In this verily are portents for people who reflect. (al-Jathiyah, 45/13)

However, this free bestowal does not mean that people can use the divine gifts however they please, without any conditions or restrictions. Indeed, in a different verse Allah declares:

Does humanity think that it is to be left aimless? (Qiyâmah, 75/36)

Thus when we spend the gifts given by Allah, we must take into account the divine orders and prohibitions. We must not forget that while unlawful spending leads to chastisement, even lawful spending requires an explanation. Just as we should keep away from unlawful acts, we should avoid committing profligacy (*isrâf*) and falling into another kind of unlawful act through our misuse of the lawful things. Indeed profligacy means to treat the gifts given by

Allah with disrespect by transgressing His limits for their employment. This is indeed an utterly ungrateful attitude towards the benefactions of Allah the Almighty.

Profligacy is a word normally applied to issues of the management of wealth, but it has a wider application that includes all kinds of affairs in which human beings may exceed rightful limits. Accordingly, if a servant exceeds the limits imposed by Allah in whatever department of life, his act constitutes profligacy. All sorts of divine gifts may be spent with no profit, but only loss.

`Iyas ﷺ said: "Anything that transgresses the limits commanded by Allah is extravagance."

Because of the workings of our egos, human beings are always inclined to think that we have good excuses for our mistakes. Even criminals who have committed the worst sorts of crimes justify their crimes and wish be excused because of various causes and motives. Both wasteful and miserly people are no different: they defend themselves with excuses, and are prone to be happy with the way they are. They are rarely free of the delusion that the madness of extravagance or the baseness of avarice constitutes true happiness. This is why the concept of profligacy, which presents itself at first sight as an empty frame, fills promptly with a picture generated by the divine commandments.

Just as profligate treatment of the material goods that are entrusted to us is prohibited by our religion; so the profligate treatment of our spiritual goods, such as creeds, acts of worship, forms of sacred knowledge, ethics, and holy times and seasons, is also prohibited. It is very possible to be wasteful and transgress limits in such affairs. Extravagance in creed is considered to be more crucial and dangerous than the others. That is because wastefulness here results in losing our eternal happiness for the sake of temporary worldly convenience.

Our Lord has prohibited both extravagance and miserliness in the treatment of all our needs, from eating, drinking, and clothing ourselves all the way up to the highest values of our spiritual lives. He has commanded us to be moderate in everything. Thus every believer must pursue the ideal of a life that strikes the balance between the two extremes. In fact, if one does not observe the divine guidelines in using material and spiritual divine gifts, one cannot avoid falling into one or the other of these two unsound situations of extravagance and miserliness.

I would like to briefly describe some of the major acts of extravagance that may lead us to calamity in the Hereafter, and indicate the way to escape them.

Wastefulness in faith and creed

This is the gravest of all kinds of wastefulness. It damages the innate disposition toward Islam built into human nature, our intellectual and spiritual dignity, by subjecting the mind to false beliefs, myths, superstitions, and pernicious trends of thought. To suffer this is to suffer the loss of eternal happiness.

Weakening of faith is a spiritual devastation that most often results from companionship with impious people. Our Lord warns us to be careful about falling into such a situation in the following verse:

And when you see those who meddle with Our revelations, withdraw from them until they meddle with another topic. And if the Devil causes you to forget, sit not, after your remembrance, in the congregation of evildoers. (al-An'âm, 6/68)

Indeed, close relationships with impious people lead to liking them, liking them leads to thinking like them, and thinking like them gradually weakens one's faith until in time eternal life itself may be lost. The causes for this kind of extravagance in one's faith are enumerated in the Qur'an as following:

From the Garden they will call to the guilty: What brought you to that Fire? They will answer: "We were not of those who prayed, nor did we feed the wretched. We used to plunge about (in vain dispute) with (other) plungers, and we denied the Day of Judgment." (al-Muddaththir, 74/40-46)

Our Lord also indicates how one may avoid such a terrible end:

O you who believe! Be careful of your duty to Allah, and be with the truthful. (at-Tawbah, 9/119)

Another Qur'anic verse reminds us of the importance of divine signs, including commands and prohibitions, and urges us to pay close attention to them so that we register their meanings in our hearts:

...and those who, when they are reminded of the revelations of their Lord, fall not deaf and blind thereat. (al-Furqân, 25/73)

The power of understanding of our eyes and our hearts are among Allah's bounties to us. To use those powers in a manner irrelevant to their purpose and thus not to see the divine signs is also a form of profligacy, since misuse lays waste to their proper function. Allah warns us about the unpleasant destiny resulting from extravagance and falsehood in the following Qur'anic verse:

....surely Allah does not guide whoever is profligate, a liar. (al-Mu'min, 40/28)

There are also cases of creedal deviation, violations of approved boundaries in belief. One of the most important common cases of creedal deviation occurs when people visit the shrines of Allah's Friends, and then direct their petitions to those Friends instead of to Allah. The appropriate way to visit Allah's Friends is to examine their sound practices during their lives, to ponder their high degree in Allah's eyes, and to ask Allah the Almighty for help out of respect for what He granted to that Friend. However, to place unconditional trust in the intercession of virtuous servants, claiming "such-and-such a virtuous servant will intervene for me and save me from punishment" is a false creed. In fact Allah declares in the Noble Qur'an that only people whom Allah permits can intercede:

On that day no intercession avails save (that of) him unto whom the All-Compassionate gives leave …. (Tâhâ, 20/109).

It is also wrong to say that virtuous servants know everything, and read people's minds and hearts. They only know whatever Allah lets them know. Otherwise, even prophets do not know all things. Accordingly, our Prophet ﷺ responded to certain questions he received by saying, "On this issue the one asked is not more knowledgeable than the one asking." Indeed, on the serious occasion of the slander of our mother A'ishah ﷞, Allah's Messenger did not receive a revelation clarifying the situation until a full month after the event. During this period, he could not make a decisive judgment about the matter. Another example is the case of the three Companions who, because of carelessness, missed joining the army assembled for the Tabuk campaign. Allah's Messenger received a revelation clarifying their situation only fifty days later.

`Uthman ibn Maz'ûn ﷞ passed away at the house of a certain Ummul-A`lâ in Madinah. Afterwards this woman declared, "O `Uthmân, I bear witness that right now Allah the Exalted is treating you well!" Allah's Messenger stopped her.

"How do you know that Allah is treating him well, right now?" he asked.

The woman said, "I swear to Allah, I do not know!"

And Allah's Messenger said, "You see that `Uthmân has died. Personally I hope that Allah shows mercy upon him. But although I am the prophet among you, I do not know what is going to happen to me or to you."

Ummu'l-Alâ related, "I swear by Allah that after that event, I never said anything about anybody (I simply hoped that my Lord would show mercy)." (Bukhârî, Tâbîr, 27)

In the Nobel Qur'an, Allah declares:

Say: I am no new thing among the Messengers (of Allah), nor know I what will be done with me or with you. I do but follow that which is revealed to me, and I am but a plain warner. (al-Ahqâf 46/9)

Somebody asked Prophet Jacob :

"O you whose heart is illuminated, the intelligent prophet! How did it happen that you smelled the scent of Joseph on a shirt that was brought all the way out of Egypt for you, yet you did not notice anything when he was lying at the bottom of a well near your own home?"

And Jacob answered, "What we receive from Allah resembles a flash of lightning.. So sometimes remote places are disclosed to us, while nearby events stay hidden!"

To offer idle compliments inattentively and for no good reason is also considered profligate, and disapproved. The Messenger of Allah said, "If any of you wants to praise your Muslim brother, and if he really has those praiseworthy attributes, then praise him like this: "I think so-and-so has such-and-such attributes. Allah is sufficient for him, I cannot guarantee anyone before Allah, but I think he is such-and-such." (Bukhârî, Shahâdât, 16)

The perfection of faith depends on a solid faculty of reason that is shaped by revelation. The perfection of reason in turn depends on the light of faith, which is maturity of heart. Those creeds and ideas deprived of divine light and instead filled with myth and superstition are like oil lamps that lack oil or light bulbs that lack electricity. Similarly, a faculty of reason that is not governed by revelation is doomed to destruction, like a light bulb that receives too much electricity or the wrong sort of current, and so gets broken.

Profligacy in ritual prayer

Moderation must characterize all acts of worship, even while ordinary dealings are so arranged as to form religiously beneficial customs. Indeed the way we accustom ourselves to do things usually determines the course of our behavior later on.

The first opportunity for extravagance in the performance of worship is the temptation to use more water than necessary in the course of the routine ritual ablution, or the full-body ritual ablution, because of needless misgivings.

Once the Messenger of Allah visited Sa'd ﷺ while the latter was performing ritual ablution. The Prophet ﷺ exclaimed, "What an extravagant use of water is this!"

Sa'd said, "How could extravagance pertain to ablution?"

The Prophet ﷺ replied, "Indeed, one may waste water even while making ablution at a flowing river!" (Ibn Mâja, Tahârah, 48)

It is among the wasteful acts to neglect to pray in congregation if one has the opportunity. It is also wasteful to pray without spiritual depth, as if discharging an unpleasant obligation. Allah says, concerning those who do not feel the awe and peace of the prayer,

So woe to the worshippers who are heedless of their prayers... (al-Mâ`ûn, 107/4-5).

The Messenger of Allah spoke about the loss of virtue in ritual prayers due to inner faults, meaning ritual prayers performed without the relevant spiritual awareness. He said, "There are those who perform the ritual prayer yet receive the reward of only half, one-third, one-fifth, one-sixth, one-seventh, one-eighth, one-ninth, or even one-tenth of its value!" (Abû Dâwûd, Salâh, 123, 124).

Allah the Almighty requires that both our minds and our hearts should be spiritually ready for worship at the time of prayer. By His command

Bow down in adoration, and bring yourself closer (to Allah)! (`Alaq, 96/19)

he demands that when our foreheads touch the ground, our hearts should be filled with humility in a state of awareness, for faith becomes perfect only when mind and heart devote themselves together, cooperating with each other. In the Qur'an, those who perform their ritual prayers properly are described:

Successful indeed are the faithful who are humble in their prayers... (Mu'minun, 23/1-2).

Another form of waste is to decrease the reward of the fast of Ramadan, which is one of the Five Pillars of Islam, by bad actions such as telling lies and talking behind people's backs. The Prophet ﷺ said, "If someone will not stop telling lies, will not stop doing business by deceiving people, then Allah will not care whether he stops eating and drinking." (Bukhârî, Sawm 8, Adab 51)

Fasting should make us better appreciate the value of the divine gifts bestowed upon us. When we stop eating and drinking for even half a day, fasting makes us grasp how weak we are. It acquaints us with the life conditions of our brothers and sisters who suffer from poor economic conditions, and encourages our hearts to become more sensitive toward them. It should also encourage us to give alms with anticipation and humility, as if we were giving alms to Allah Himself. Indeed the Qur'an says:

....Allah accepts the repentance of His servants and receives their gifts of charity... (Tawbah 9/104).

The holy month of Ramadan, when fasting is obligatory, is full of light, spirituality, mercy, forgiveness, and the effects of divine favor. The Messenger of Allah urged us to benefit from the divine enlightenment and grace active during Ramadan as much as we possibly can. In the nights of Ramadan we should perform the routine prayers with full concentration, asking Allah for forgiveness, remembering Him, reflecting upon His attributes, and reciting the holy Qur'an. In the days we should continue worshipping with fullness of heart by giving alms and undertaking good deeds. At the time of breaking the fast, which is when Allah accepts the prayers of His servants, we should enjoy the peace that results from asking Allah for forgiveness, praising Him, and supplying food to our fellow Muslims for the Ramadan dinner. In the evening we should use our time wisely by pursuing proper performance of the special Ramadan prayers. If we cannot utilize this holy month properly, we will have missed receiving benefit from a sea of divine mercy and forgiveness right there next to us, and so will have simply wasted other gifts we have received.

There is profligacy in Pilgrimage when a would-be pilgrim does not care whether he earns his living by lawful means; when he pays no attention to the rights of other people over him; when he busies himself with futile activities and engages in acts that set spiritual grace and enlightenment at a distance. All these count as wastefulness. In fact, the Messenger of Allah said of the profligate pilgrim, "When he shouts "*Labbayk!*," (The pilgrims' cry, "O my Lord, I am at your service!") he is answered, "You have nothing to do with that cry, or anything like it! Your earnings are unlawful, your food is unlawful, your transportation is unlawful. Go back as a sinner, without any reward! Be sad, for you will encounter things that you do not like!" (Haythamî, III, 209-210).

Profligacy appears in almsgiving and charity when one troubles the needy by reminding them of one's generosity. If a person should be infected with spiritual diseases of the heart such as hypocrisy and pride, the result will be wastefulness in giving.. Allah says in the noble Qur'an:

Kind words and the covering of faults are better than charity followed by injury. ..... O you who believe! cancel not your charity by reminders of your generosity or by injury.... (Baqarah, 2/263-264).

Every believer should carefully search out persons who deserve to receive alms. Indeed Allah praises people who undertake such an inquiry as

...those who are active in deeds of charity... (Mu'minun, 23/4).

To deliver monetary alms and charity goods to people who really deserve them is extremely important. Allah commands us to do research in this regard and develop the skills "to recognize the needy by their faces."[33] Certainly, our ability to deliver support to people to whom it is due depends on our own means of livelihood. The alms we spend and the charity we give will reveal to us, like a truthful mirror,

198

33. See, Baqara 2/273.

whether our earnings were lawfully obtained. If we earn the money lawfully, it will be well spent on good and deserving people. If it is earned unlawfully, then it will be wasted on undeserving people.

There is wastefulness in Qur'an recitation if one makes no effort to recite it properly or to understand its message, and if one remains indifferent to the orders and prohibitions stated in it. Such a person is profligate regarding a great and precious treasure. Allah distinguishes those who are profligate and those who fully benefit from the light of the Qur'an in the following verse:

We have given the Book as inheritance to such of Our servants as we have chosen. Among them are some who wrong their own souls; some who follow a middle course; and some who are, by Allah's leave, foremost in good deeds. That is the highest grace. (Fâtir, 35/32).

Just as the most privileged of human beings are the community of the Prophet Muhammad ﷺ, so the most elevated people of this community are those who recite the Qur'an, learn it by heart, absorb its messages, and follow the rules it provides. Some people wrong themselves: they do not recite the Qur'an and do not follow its guidance despite having had the opportunity to study. This is simply wasting a great gift. Some people follow a middle path, since they practice it at times, and leave it aside at times. Some others, however, by Allah's permission, excel in good deeds.

The noble Qur'an is the language of the heavens and the earth. It is a blessing for souls and a treasure of spirituality. It is a miracle of expression dedicated to humanity. Every heart that fully absorbs it becomes a site of divine manifestation. Those who assimilate the generous Qur'an experience unique peace of mind and happiness, for the Qur'an is a micro cosmos embracing the whole universe in its magnificence. For the people of heart, the glorious Qur'an is like a splendid door providing access to the depths of the world of contemplation.

In order to recite the Qur'an properly, purity of heart is as important as cleanliness of body. There are spiritual diseases of the heart that prevent people from encountering the Qur'an in an appropriate manner. Those who cannot receive the divine mercy, cure, and guidance in it end up in a condition of great loss. Since the Qur'an expresses the will of Allah, it can be understood best by pious and virtuous people. In order to be able to benefit from the bounty of the generous Qur'an and thus obtain happiness in this world as well as in the Hereafter, one must attain *taqwa*, or mindfulness of Allah.

Another issue requiring attention is the service of human beings. To serve others for Allah's sake, even in unimportant things, may be more valuable than much supererogatory prayer. The following case from the Age of Felicity explains this precisely.

One time when he was traveling, the Prophet ﷺ encamped at a suitable place. Some of his Companions were fasting, so they fell asleep immediately, since they were quite tired. Others brought water to be used for ablution and set up tents for shelter. When the time to break the fast arrived, the Prophet ﷺ said, "Today, those who did not fast acquired more reward (than those who fasted)." (Muslim, Sıyâm, 100-101).

If a person occupies himself with secondary things and neglects earning his livelihood so that he becomes needy, this is also a kind of extravagance. Indeed, the Prophet ﷺ stated, "Allah the Almighty loves to see a servant who grows tired working for lawful livelihood." (as-Suyûtî, al-Jâmi` as-Saghîr, I, 65).

Another kind of profligacy appears when people make supplications to Allah in a group. Some people will pray at extravagant length, especially when praying in public. They may even shout so as to indicate a special gift, perhaps uttering rhyming expressions. Such performances cause the community to lose interest. All this amounts to no more than wasting the essence of worship. In fact the Messenger of Allah prohibited making supplications in a screaming and shouting manner: "Do not scream when you pray to Allah. You are not addressing one who is deaf!" (Bukhârî, Jihâd, 131; Muslim, Dhikr, 44). Such immoderate petitions result in the destruction of the spirituality of pious acts.

Profligacy in worship eliminates its benefits. In a different hadith of the Prophet 鸞, we read, "A group will emerge out of this community who will transgress the limits of purification and prayer." (Abû Dâwûd, Tahârah, 45).

To sum up, Allah the Almighty warns us against performing ritual acts automatically, unconsciously, without seeking the enlightenment and deep engagement to be drawn from them. Allah asks our hearts to come closer to Him. They approach Him as they become filled with spirituality and illumination through a sense of divine blessings received. Allah wants our hearts to reach divine encounter.

O our Lord! May you protect us from wastefulness in faith, creeds and ritual either by neglecting them or by transgressing rightful limits! May you bestow upon us all the sublime taste and excitement acquired through perfecting our faith, and the peace and pleasure resulting from the living performance of ritual acts!

Amin…

CHAPTER 13

Wastefulness - 2
Concerning Time

Life is an extremely valuable bounty bestowed by Allah upon every living thing once only, and for a limited period of time. Thus it is necessary to spend time on actions that suit its value. There are always different things that might be done with every moment.

You cannot borrow any time, or lend any to others… It is possible to buy almost anything, but it is never possible to buy back time that has passed.

CHAPTER 13

WASTEFULNESS – 2

Concerning Time

All the bounties received by human beings, whether through our own efforts or freely bestowed, are blessings granted by Allah the Almighty. This is because it is Allah the Almighty who creates all these bounties in the first place, and it is He who creates the abilities and powers that servants need in order to obtain them. We must never forget that we are the recipients of divine blessing. We must pursue our live without ever losing track of the knowledge that all these bounties are items given in trust, about which we shall be questioned one day. The noble Qur'an clearly states it:

Did you then think that We had created you in vain, and that you should not be returned to Us? (Mu'minûn, 23/115).

So when we make use of the material or spiritual property we possess, we must be aware that we are not unaccountable. We should utilize whatever is at our disposal so as to merit divine consent.

In another verse in the noble Qur'an, our Lord reminds us of the great interrogation and underlines that we bear a responsibility:

Then on that day you shall most certainly be questioned about the profit. (Takâthur, 102/8)

Allah regulates how we may acquire the bounties He bestows. He also regulates the ways we may use them. These rules establish the difference between lawful and unlawful things. Extravagance is counted among the things that cause loss of divine mercy and love, and attract divine wrath. In the noble Qur'an, Allah declares:

...and be not prodigal. Lo! Allah loves not the prodigals. (An`âm, 6/141)

Profligacy in the use of time

Wasting time is one of the gravest mistakes that people are prone to. It is a result of inattentiveness and forgetfulness. Life is an extremely valuable bounty bestowed by Allah upon every living thing once only, and for a limited period of time. Thus it is necessary to spend time on actions that suit its value. There are always different things that might be done with every moment. However, the guiding principle is to give priority to whatever is most important now. We should then order whatever follows according to each thing's level of importance.

For instance, for a mother to give priority to nursing her baby is proper, since that is a behavior required by her mercy and compassion toward her baby. However, if she should persist in nursing the child while her apartment is on fire, she would be showing stupidity and would incur a heavy responsibility. At that moment, her priority is to try to put out the fire. If she were to take it easy and do nothing while the apartment burned, in a short while she and her baby too would be destroyed by the fire.

Similarly, because of the fragile character of this era, it is among our responsibilities to use our time to try to make the religion of Allah stronger.

The noble Companions of the Prophet, who were extremely careful about their use of time, felt that the best time they spent was the period when they were occupied with carrying the divine message to other people. One of the Prophet's Companions was about to be executed by nonbelievers. The person responsible for the execution allowed three minutes for this Companion's last wish. The Companion thanked the unfortunate man and said, "So it seems that I have three more minutes to explain Islam to you. I hope you find guidance."

In today's world, clearly some people are lost to the erosion of unbelief and immorality. Given this situation, it is incumbent upon every believer, because of our faith and conscience, to reach out to such people with gentle and conciliatory words and let them know the beauty and kindness of Islam.

To behave wastefully when making use of time, that extremely valuable capital, by engaging in futile and pointless activities, may endanger the life of the Hereafter. For people who have drawn aside the veil of ignorance, time is an incomparable bounty, unlike anything else. In Surah 'Asr, (Time), Allah the Almighty says:

By (the Token of) Time (through the ages), verily humanity is in loss, except those who have faith and do righteous deeds, and join together (in the mutual teaching) of truth, and of perseverance. ('Asr, 103/1-3)

This chapter, which begins with an oath sworn on Time, declares that times lived without faith or not employed in doing good and joining together in advising truth and patience, are simply lost. They are occasions of disappointment. Those who utilize their time properly are indicated to be exceptions to the human rule. Thus the chapter implies the bitter truth that the majority of people fail in regard to time.

Allah the Almighty gives the following advice to His servants so that they may escape from the disappointments of time and may receive divine blessings:

Therefore, when you are free (from your immediate task), still labor hard, and to your Lord turn (all) your attention. (Inshirâh, 94/7-8)

That is, one must turn immediately from one good work to the next. We should not allow even a moment to pass without investing it in worship and good deeds. For time is a treasure lent to us so that we may acquire happiness in the Hereafter, and death is the deadline for the repayment of our debt.

A businessman takes out a loan with a promise to pay back his debt at a definite time. The time is fixed so that the indebted person may prepare for the payment. Our worldly life is the time allotted us to prepare for the life of the Hereafter, so that we might perhaps acquire divine acceptance. If a businessman does not take the deadline seriously and does not prepare for it, he will suffer difficulties when his debt falls due..And if human beings do not use the time allotted us properly, we Weill be unable to escape from disappointment. Every person is destined to assume responsibility for a fixed period beginning immediately at birth. At the end of that period, each of us will meet Azrael 🕊, the angel of death. And although it is certain that the debt of human life will fall due, our due date is unknown. This tremendous situation urges us at all times to be ready to pay over our lives.

The reality that life is a divine bounty to be properly utilized is the basis of an important Sufi principle, known as *wuquf-i zamâni,* "remaining present with the time." According to this concept, a person of faith who aims at cleaning his soul and purifying his heart must engage in conscious and appropriate good acts from moment to moment, and examine himself all the time. He must leave what is unnecessary, and keep away from idle talk. As Mawlânâ Jalâluddîn Rûmî tells us, such a person must protect his tongue from being a "clown of words." Indeed, this is how Allah describes those servants who obtain salvation:

They shun vain and useless affairs. (Mu'minun, 23/3).

…When they pass by senseless words and useless things, they pass by with dignity. (Furqân, 25/72)

A virtuous believer must always be aware of his inner world. He should consider how he asks Allah for pardon, how he thanks Allah, and how content he is with his life. He should reflect on the endless bounties he receives and on his gratitude for them, and he must repent for the time he has spent in ignorance. He should keep clear of the ignorance of his past, and set himself free from pointless worries about the future. He must strive to fulfill the requirements of the moment he is living. That is, he must be "the son of the moment" – he must fully appreciate the value of his life and especially the moment he is experiencing now.

A mature believer will spend his time in preparation for the life of the Hereafter. In fact, wasting our precious life on vanities is one of the chief causes of regret. The Messenger of Allah ﷺ said, "The people of Paradise shall regret nothing but time spent during worldly life without the remembrance Allah!" (Haythamî, X, 73-74). Thus he reminds us that believers must invest their time like capital to reap an endless life. When opportunities are lost, remorse is of no avail.. Hence we must spend our lives properly while we have the chance. We must strive to thank Allah as much as we can with every capacity of our natures. For example, we should make efforts to thank Allah for the divine gift of the tongue by praising Him with the recitation of litanies, which is the cure for the heart.

The Prophet ﷺ advised his wife, the Mother of the Believers, Hafsah ﷺ: "O Hafsah! Beware of talking too much. Too much talk without the mention of Allah kills the heart. But mention Allah frequently, because it revives the heart." (Ali al-Muttaqî, I, 439/1896)

Allah the Almighty warns us:

...Spend something (in charity) out of the substance We have bestowed upon you before Death come to any of you, that he should say, "O my Lord! Would that you gave me respite for a little while! I should then have given (largely) in charity, and I should have been one of the doers of good." (al-Munâfiqûn 63/10)

The following Qur'anic verse, which relates the cries and excuses of those who end up in disappointment, is quite remarkable:

Therein will they cry aloud for assistance: "Our Lord! Bring us out: we shall work righteousness, not the (deeds) we used to do!" And Allah will say to them: "Did We not give you long enough life so that he that would, should receive admonition? And (moreover) the warner came to you. So taste the chastisement!" For the wrongdoers there is no helper. (Fâtir, 35/37)

The major cause leading to wastefulness concerning time is that people do not clearly grasp death, and keep assuming that it is far away from them. This is certainly a foundation of ignorance, and is responsible for the waste of other bounties, too. Indeed in the Prophetic tradition we read, "Remember death often! It uproots all kinds of pleasure." (Tirmidhî, Qıyâmah, 26). All behaviors that remain indifferent to the Prophetic warning will lead to chastisement one day.

One day the Messenger of Allah said: "There is nobody who will die and not be regretful."

His noble Companions then asked: "How can all people be regretful?"

And the Prophet ﷺ replied: "If he is a pious person, then he will regret not having performed more good deeds. And if he is an evildoer, then he will regret not having abandoned evil actions." (Tirmidhî, Zuhd, 59).

When a person carefully considers the effects of divine power in himself or in the cosmos, looking with the eyes of the heart, he feels compelled to think about how he should pursue his life. Death is the most visible event that affects the direction of anyone's life. That tremendous moment of farewell is full of lessons to be pondered. Anyone who is aware of what death is will not be deceived by temporary pleasures; anyone who knows that he is a passenger traveling toward the Hereafter cannot be taken in by the toys in this worldly hotel. He will not spend his time playing with them. In the noble Qur'an, Allah declares:

We created not the heavens, the earth, and all that is between them merely in sport. We created them not except for truth. But most of them do not understand. (Dukhân, 44/38-39)

Even if we received every transitory bounty and lived for a thousand years, it would all come to nothing in the end. Isn't our destination under the soil that is beneath our feet? Why do we not take heed of the fact that the youth and the strength of all mortal beings has always been ground up by the mill of time? It would be utterly horrible, with regard to the endless future life, if one tried to hang on to the flattery that feeds raw egos in a world unlinked to the Hereafter, if one took the toys of this playpen to be anything real!... Imam Shafi`î asks: "Would it be intelligent for caravans on the move to build houses on the road?"

211

Think of those who immerse themselves in worldly pleasures with the aim of achieving peace of mind without taking the Hereafter into account. It is certainly a saddening waste of one's life. It is a painful loss! Those who fritter away their time as if they will never die, will regret their behavior and sorely miss their lost time later.

People identified with their carnal desires always try to avoid thinking about death and what is beyond it so that their heedless lives may continue uninterrupted.. But death will swallow them anyway. The prospect produces great anxiety about the future, and ultimately becomes a terrifying nightmare. All of us want to live in an imaginary world constructed according to our own preferences. But would an intelligent person trade reality for fantasy, a palace for a ruin? It is clear that there are many people who ruin their life in the Hereafter while aiming to improve their life in this world.

Mawlânâ Jalâluddîn Rûmî points out the way to escape from the worldly prison and achieve the endless happiness. He said, "Don't hold fast to properties and possessions, so that you may easily leave them when you have to. And if you can easily leave a thing behind, you might as well leave it and earn the reward! Cling to the One who holds you fast: that is the First and the Last." He also said, "The majority of people fear that their bodies shall die. But the thing that deserves to be feared is the death of hearts."

There is a designated end for the life of all animate things. This designated end cannot be eliminated, or postponed for awhile so as to extend the course of worldly life. Time goes by, as is commanded by divine law. You cannot borrow any time, or lend any to others. In this world, it is possible to buy almost anything, but it is never possible to buy back time that has passed.

Yet though nobody remains indifferent when a gold coin is thrown out in the garbage, still many people care nothing when time is thrown away on futile things.

Fariduddîn Attâr ⬚ remarked: "There are four things that cannot be reclaimed: a word that has left the mouth, an arrow that has left the bow, an accident that has already happened, and a life that has been spent in vain."

One of Allah's Friends gave us the following advice: "Go and visit hospitals once in a while! Then you will thank Allah because you are free from the pain and diseases the patients suffer; you have received the bounty of health. Go and visit prisons once in a while! Reflect upon the pain-filled lives of the prisoners. Notice that crimes are committed in just a moment, out of ignorance or psychological disorder. Think about the fact that sometimes people are wrongfully incarcerated and suffer for crimes they never committed. Think about the possibility that you could be one of them! Then thank Allah, since He has protected you from falling into such miserable situations. Praise Allah for your well-being. Then go and visit grave-yards once in a while. Listen to the soundless cries and screams; understand the silent speech. Know that remorse is useless once life is over, and so learn the value of your time. Recite a prayer for the people of the graves, and try hard to spend your days filled with thanking Allah and praising Him with recitation of His names!"

Thus the faithful must make efforts to live always in remem-brance of Allah the Almighty. Indeed Allah says in the holy Qur'an:

And be not like those who forgot Allah, therefore He caused them to forget their own souls. Such are the evildoers. (Hashr, 59/19)

Abû Abdur-Rahman as-Sulamî states that wasting time and keeping company with those who have no concerns beyond this worldly life are among the gravest faults of the soul. He then explains how such faults can be eliminated: "One should consider time the most valuable thing and use it accordingly. i.e., That is, one should continuously praise Allah with remembrance, always be in a state of worship, and keep on trying to establish sincerity in one's soul. The Messenger of Allah said: "One sign of a mature Muslim is that a person leaves aside things that do not concern him." (Tirmidhi, Zuhd, 11)."

Among the Prophetic traditions we find the following statements:

• "Value five things before the occurrence of five other things: youth before the occurrence of age, health before the occurrence of sickness, wealth before the occurrence of poverty, leisure before the occurrence of labor, and life before the occurrence of death!" (Hâkim, Mustadrak, IV, 341; Bukhârî, Riqaq, 3; Tirmidhî, Zuhd, 25).

• "After the Resurrection, the feet of a servant will be unable to move before he is questioned about four things. (1) His life: how did he use it? (2) His youth: how did he occupy it? (3) His wealth: how did he gain it, how spend it? (4) His knowledge: what did he do with it? (Tirmidhî, Qıyâma, 1).

• "There are two gifts: most people are deceived about their use. They are health and spare time." (Bukhârî, Riqaq, 1).

Allah the Almighty declares frequently in the Qur'an that he shall hold us responsible in the Hereafter for both the material and the spiritual bounties we have received. Muslim scholars have arrived at different answers to the question of which are the most crucial gifts for which we must account. Ibn Mas'ûd ﷺ argued that they are "security, health, and leisure." Mu'âwiya ibn Qurra ﷺ said that "the severest accounting on the Day of Judgment is the accounting of spare time." (Bursawî, X, 504).

Imam al-Ghazalî warned, "O my son! Suppose that you died today. You would grieve for the time you had spent heedlessly. You would say "If only…" But it would all be over!"

Hadrat Junayd al-Baghdadi said: "One day in the world is more valuable than a thousand years in the Hereafter. That is because both earning things and losing them belong to this world. In the Hereafter we can neither earn nor lose."

Time spent in vain is a painful loss that cannot be restored. All files belonging to the past are closed. However, we may still strive to restore the loss at the spiritual level by praying to Allah, asking His forgiveness, and taking refuge in Him as we regret our wasted time.

The river of life flows fast. The fleeting days making up our lives, numbered by the divine will, are like drops filling a cup. Each day we advance toward the endpoint; we move away from the world and draw closer to the grave. Since we do not when we will depart, we should keep in the mind that we can come across Azrael ﷺ at any time, accordingly we should be ready at any moment to breathe out our last breath.

If we think carefully, we will discover that the future is open to good news as well as to dangers. And we do not know how many leaves are left in the calendar of our life..

May Allah the Almighty grant us, as he declared in the holy Qur'an, that we may worship Him until *what is certain* – which is death – *comes upon us*, [34] so that we die as Muslims.[35] May Allah grant that we pursue lives free of extravagance, established in moderation, and harmoniously balanced in the inner and outer worlds May we ornament His bounty Time with good and beautiful deeds!

Amin…

---

34. See Hijr, 15/99.
35. See Âl İmrân, 3/102

CHAPTER 14

Wastefulness - 3

Concerning Knowledge

The spirit that will give shape to societies is not the spirit of selfish pedants who memorize large numbers of books, but the spirit of those who deepen their hearts with wisdom drawn from the Qur'an and who are a source of mercy and peace for society. That is the spirit of people mindful of Allah, the faithful who love serving others.

To know is to solve the secret of creation, to be familiar with wisdom, and to possess a heart competent to receive its share from the disclosure of divine majesty and the flow of divine power.

WASTEFULNESS – 3

Concerning Knowledge

In order for our life to acquire depth, elegance, and meaning, and thus become beautiful, we must avoid wastefulness and other negative qualities. In fact, wastefulness is the forerunner of the destruction in the individual and the family, as well as in society.

All the bounties bestowed upon us are trusts. If they are not delivered to their proper places but are squandered in heedlessness and lust, Allah the Almighty removes his blessing.

Profligacy should not be thought of as merely the waste of property and possessions: it is a danger in all areas of life. We have seen that spending one's life in vain is a kind of profligacy. Occupying oneself with useless knowledge, and misuse of knowledge for selfish reasons, are also profligate behavior.

The pursuit of knowledge is a sacred activity that satisfies the wonder produced in us by creation: such is the human desire to learn. That desire represents the apex of human nature. It is the love of knowledge that leads the faithful to wish to know Allah the Almighty, to thank Him, and to exalt Him by ritual acts.

The noblest form of knowledge is the personal knowledge of Allah (*ma'rifat Allâh*), which is the ability to recognize Allah in one's heart. This transitory world resembles a classroom where an examination is being held. Under the circumstances, to busy oneself with knowledge that does not lead to the recognition of Allah, that does not ultimately produce wisdom and nurture the encounter with Truth in the heart, is a waste of the human drive to learn.

In the noble Qur'an, authentic knowledge is accompanied by deep feeling, namely mindfulness and surrender to Allah. We read:

Is he who offers devotions in the watches of the night, prostrate and standing, mindful of the Hereafter and hoping for the mercy of his Lord, (to be accounted equal with a disbeliever)? Say (unto them, O Muhammad): Are those who know equal with those who know not? But only people of understanding will pay heed. (az-Zumar, 39/9).

If we consider this verse carefully, we can differentiate knowledge and ignorance using divine criteria. Should we wish to be among those who know wisdom and truth, we should observe the following conditions:

1. During the night we should pray to Allah the Almighty, prostrate and standing, so that our hearts feel present with Him.

2. At every moment, in the course of all states and behaviors, we should be conscious of the accounting in the Hereafter.

3. We should constantly take refuge in our Lord, hoping for His mercy.

4. We should pursue a life guided by mindfulness of Allah, and so draw closer to Him.

5. We should protect ourselves from negative attributes that push one away from Allah the Almighty. We should make an effort to manifest the attributes of beauty, cultivating beautiful character traits in ourselves, particularly generosity.

6. We should maintain an awareness of being under divine observation, for it is as if all our actions are recorded by divine cameras.

7. We should try our best to protect our hearts from greed and worldly ambition .

8. We should be patient when difficulties arise concerning the implementation of religious rules and the communication of religious teachings.

If we would like to avoid being among "those who do not know," here are their attributes.

1. Faithlessness and ingratitude.

2. Asking Allah for help in times of difficulty, but forgetting about Him in times of ease.

3. Setting up something else as equal to Allah, with the intention of leading people astray or as a result of indulging one's selfish desires. Certainly Allah says:

Have you seen him who chose for his god his own lust? (Furqân, 43).

All of the sciences consist of discovering the rules and laws established by Allah to govern beings and events. Advancement in science depends upon increasing such discoveries. However, identifying the rules and laws established by Allah to govern beings and events is not the knowledge that leads servants to wisdom. That sacred and most desirable kind of knowledge consists of more than simple observation.

The most desirable knowledge results in our understanding the reasons behind our coming to this world and our departing from it. It encompasses understanding the language of all beings, and discovering their secrets. To know in this way is to solve the secret of creation, to be familiar with wisdom, and to possess a heart competent to receive its share from the disclosure of divine majesty and the flow of divine power.

To know is to find that which is really necessary. And the noble Qur'an states that the most necessary of all things is to die in a state of surrender to Allah.[36]

To know is to set oneself free from the slavery of the animal self before it dies, and to awaken to the dawn of truth. To know is to interrogate ourselves before Allah does it for us.

Mawlânâ Jalâluddîn Rûmî dove into the ocean of divine knowledge through deepening his understanding of outward religious knowledge. He spoke of his lifetime as divided into three stages. He characterized the early period, when he reached the zenith of the exoteric sciences but did not taste the pleasure of being closer to Truth, by saying "I was raw." He characterized the middle period, when he received the disclosures of wisdom in his heart and reached divine pleasure, by saying "I was cooked." And he characterized the period of maturity, when the secrets in the cosmos became readable like a book, by saying, "I am burnt."

Spiritual sensitivity increases with advancing knowledge. True knowledge makes a person a traveler through a valley of wonders. The more one gets to know the wisdom and truth built into the cosmos, the more one becomes aware of the fact that one is weak, limited, and useless by oneself.. That realization is self-knowledge, and whoever knows himself, knows his Lord.

• One, who knows, knows the true owner of creation, the king of the only kingdom. Such a person becomes an abundant source of tenderness and mercy to creatures, because of their Creator.

---

36. See Âl-Imrân, 3/102

• One who knows, forgives; one who knows, perseveres; one who knows, loves. One who knows seeks the good pleasure of his Lord and intimacy with Him. For such a person, self-sacrifice is joy.

• One who knows does not hurt others and cannot be hurt by others. Such people are emotionally very strong and do not live under the influence of unconscious feelings. Their language is the language of compassion.

• One who knows, if she has to choose between pleasing Allah and pleasing His servants, chooses the good pleasure of Allah.

• One who knows tries to be with the One, his Lord, in every situation – "*standing up, sitting down, or lying on his side.*"[37]

• One who knows always engages in contemplation, is aware of the divine magnificence and the flow of divine power through the universe. Politeness, elegance, and sensitivity become his essential nature.

• One who knows is a person of heart and spirituality.

• One who knows finds peace and happiness everywhere and in any situation.

• One who knows feels responsible for other people and for society.

• One who knows is aware of the fact that her country, nation, and flag are all entrusted to him. This is because protection of faith, family, property, and life all depend on the protection of the country and the nation from destructive influences.

---

37. See Âl-Imrân, 3/191.

• One who knows commits himself to the spiritual life in order to become free from the slavery of the animal self.

• One who knows is set free from playing with the deceitful toys of the transitory world. He keeps her fleeting possessions out of her heart.

• One who knows sets himself free from rudeness of heart, from the evils of fame and lust.

• One who knows has such maturity of heart that when he encounters the attractive invitations of wealth, fame, and desire, she is able to say "I take refuge in Allah."[38]

• One who knows understands his nothingness before the divine majesty. One who knows, knows that he does not know anything.

• One who knows gets rid of foolishness and is aware of what he should know.

• One who knows experiences the pleasure of showing mercy, serving others, and being humble, for these are the fruits of having faith, and he experiences the taste of faith.

• One who knows, marvels at beauty. That is, he admires the wonderful examples of divine art in the cosmos.

• One who knows understands the language of the universe, because everything talks to the one who knows.

• One who knows experiences the harmony between the intuitions of the intellect and those of the heart.

• One who knows constantly experiences the love and ecstasy flowing from faith.

---

38. See Yusuf, 12/23.

• One who knows has a share in direct personal knowledge of Allah.

• One who knows moves from the cause to the Causer, from the effect to the Effective, from the art to the Absolute Artist.

• One who knows his Lord in his heart knows everything. One who does not know Him cannot know anything, for people become foolish when their hearts are blind.

The Messenger of Allah, who is the best among those who know the Lord, said, "If you knew what I know, you would laugh seldom and cry often…You would go out to the desert and pray to Allah with fervent cries." (Ibn Mâja, Zuhd, 19).

When ʿUmar , the second caliph, passed away, Abdullah ibn Masʿûd remarked, "Nine -tenths of knowledge has now departed."

Other Companions objected. "There are still knowledgeable people among us!" they observed.

But Ibn Masʿûd answered, "I am talking about inner knowledge, not outer knowledge."

In the noble Qur'an, Allah declares:

…among His servants, only people of knowledge fear Allah. (Fâtir, 35/28)

As the holy verse indicates, knowledge that does not evoke the feeling of surrender and the fear of Allah in one's heart is not the kind of knowledge that meets with Allah's good pleasure, the merits of which are mentioned in the Qur'an and in Prophetic traditions.

Certainly, the worldly sciences are needed insofar as they are used properly. Indeed, the worldly sciences, through their progress, have provided human understanding with new evidences of the magnificence of Allah. Thus they contribute to human appreciation of the splendor of the divine art and its wonderful disclosure. In this regard, the undertakings of science, from astrophysics to genetics to the wonders achieved by technology, indeed all the scholarly activities and their applications, serve the discovery of the flow of divine power in the cosmos.

In the noble Qur'an, Allah states:

We shall show them Our signs on the horizons and in themselves until it is clear to them that it is the truth. Does not your Lord suffice as witness over all things? (Fussilat, 41/53)

The point of seeking knowledge is to learn the secrets of the physical and metaphysical realms so as to reach deeper understanding of Allah. That is, in addition to affirming the existence of the Creator, one's heart should be capable of seeing how divine power flows through things and how Allah's might is disclosed in them. What a pity some hearts are so sick with ignorance that they cannot grasp the divine art despite all the advancement in sciences and so many discoveries!

Those who commit injustice by misusing knowledge for personal advantage are indeed unfaithful to knowledge itself. This means that they are wasteful of their own minds and hearts. In order for any knowledge to become useful, the intellect and will that produce it must be educated by Qur'anic and Prophetic teachings. Then the results of the search for knowledge may cure the raw egotism and weaknesses from which mankind suffers. If a scholar lacks such an education in religious principles, his knowledge may lead him into dangerous paths so that he becomes a means of leading people astray.

Unfortunately, today when students are examined to determine whether they can pursue advanced studies, the only accepted criterion is their mental abilities. No one bothers with asking whether a student has the virtues and merits of heart that will enable him to assume the responsibilities of the science he wishes to learn. Yet in order to obtain eternal happiness and salvation, studying something externally is not sufficient.

Take for example the case of a student of law. If his study is not guided by spiritual knowledge, he may support injustice and cruelty with his legal knowledge, instead of supporting right and justice. Or take a student of medicine: she may turn out to be a professional killer instead of helping people to recover! A manager with the mental capacity for learning business, if he lacks the feeling of mercy and love, may end up as a tyrant over his employees. Through their professional knowledge, such people may cause much more harm than uneducated people are capable of producing.. And if they use their knowledge wrongfully and wastefully, they may be destined to eternal disappointment.

Mawlânâ Jalâluddîn Rûmî ﷺ clarifies this point in his *Mathnawî*:

A talented person may be envied. But take heed of the case of the Devil, and (if your knowledge is not in harmony with your heart) do not be too impressed with yourself. Don't forget that the condemned Iblîs, cast away from the divine mercy, was one of the closest beings to Allah for thousands of years: he was the chief of the angels. Yet he became proud of his knowledge and worship, and so behaved badly, taking issue with the creation of Adam ﷺ. Iblis despised Adam, and as a result he was disgraced.

If the knowledge you acquire guides you to truth, to reality, to mindfulness, and to good deeds, then it is genuine knowledge. We should not forget that the Devil had knowledge, and that Qârûn (who set up the Golden Calf) had knowledge as well. But their knowledge inflated their egos and led them to extreme pride and arrogance. They could not control the desires originating from their lower selves, and they trusted themselves too much.

Certainly, knowledge that leads people to boastful display and arrogance and thus to disappointment may outwardly produce beautiful and useful things. Is it not a grave responsibility? This is why when the Messenger of Allah prayed to Allah for knowledge, he always said: "O my Lord! I ask You for useful knowledge! I take refuge in You from useless knowledge!.. (Muslim, Dhikr, 73).

There are different kinds of useful knowledge. Just as knowledge of basic Islamic practice (*fiqh*) is indispensable, so knowledge concerning turning to Allah, sincerity, and avoiding hypocrisy is also indispensable. If one neglects the latter, one may be disappointed in the Hereafter. Those who do not obtain the most useful knowledge, no matter how many other things they know, may be deprived of reaching the only Truth, our Lord.

Imam Ghazâlî warns against the waste of time and effort when studying sciences:

The sciences that you study should be such that they illuminate your heart and beautify your character. Suppose you knew that you had only one week left in your life. Immediately, and for the rest of that limited time, you would turn to useful knowledge. You would meditate on your situation, cut your ties to worldly desires and try to be the best person you could be. But it is certain that on any night or any day we live, we may possibly die. Accordingly, the studies that you prefer to engage should be such that they make you sensitive regarding the divine greatness and guide you to enhance your spirituality.

The acquisition of knowledge requires suffering difficulties, yet its value only emerges when it is implemented in life. Acquiring knowledge but not implementing it is meaningless labor under the burden of useless weight. It turns a scholar into a porter, or as the Qur'an says, "*a donkey carrying books.*"[39] If knowledge is not well digested and put into practice, if it does not influence our behavior, if it does not become part of our personality and reach the level of recognition of Allah, if it does not direct the servant toward self-effacement, humility, and the elimination of arrogance, then it is immoderate and all the effort spent acquiring it is wasted.

One should not forget that Allah the Almighty entrusted all truths and secrets to humanity in the noble Qur'an. The essence of all sciences is contained in it. Whatever is found in the cosmos, "*dry or moist,*" (An'am, 6/59) has a place in the Qur'anic treasury. Allah the Almighty says:

The All-Compassionate has taught the Qur'an. He has created the human being. He has taught him speech. (Rahmân, 55/1-4).

The Qur'an consists of the latest instructions and messages of Allah the Almighty to humanity. The kind of knowledge that our nation and world need the most, today, is the kind of knowledge found in the Qur'an. This is why we must pay attention to learning it properly. However, in order to understand the Qur'an properly, one must enter into its realm of spirituality, and one must have the property of mindfulness, which is an attitude of heart. Indeed the Qur'an warns believers:

...when they are reminded of the revelations of their Lord, they do not fall deaf and blind thereat. (Furqân, 25/73).

---

39. See Jum'ah, 62/5

...And verily we have struck for humanity in this Qur'an all kinds of similitudes, that perhaps they may reflect (az-Zumar, 39/27).

Thus the Qur'an urges us to form a profound relationship with it. But in order to establish such a relationship, it is necessary for us to purify our hearts as we purify our bodies for worship. And for that, we need spiritual education. We also read in the Qur'an:

Will they not then meditate on the Qur'an? Or are there locks on their hearts? (Muhammad, 47/24)

Truly he succeeds who purifies it (his inner being, from bad character traits) (Shams, 91/9).

Our guide, the noble Qur'an, invites us to reflection. Since the noble Qur'an announces the divine will, some people, those who are spiritually closer to Allah the Almighty, will grasp its message better that others. Nut as it is stated in the noble Qur'an:

...So fear Allah; Allah teaches you... (Baqarah, 2/282).

This is why every verse in the Qur'an is open to us according to the level to which our heart belongs.

In the noble Qur'an, Allah warns the whole Muslim community in the person of the Prophet ﷺ :

...if you follow their wishes after knowledge has come to you, then truly you shall have from Allah no protecting friend nor defender. (Ra`d, 13/37)

The fact that our Lord describes the noble Qur'an as "knowledge" indicates that for Muslims the first imperative of study is the Qur'an, and culture based on the Qur'an. No authentic Muslim intellectual life without reference to the Qur'an can be conceived. Unfortunately, some people in our time have demoted the study of the noble Qur'an to a subsidiary affair.

It is quite sad that some believers think that the Qur'anic education we provide our children need not be serious and long. They prefer short programs like summer schools or weekend courses, as if they were trying to dispose of an unwanted burden! Parents also neglect the dimension of meaning in their children's Qur'anic education. They tend to put emphasis simply on the recitation of the Qur'an, but not on the instructions in the Qur'an.

To undervalue the noble Qur'an, the greatest divine gift to humanity, and belittle the Qur'anic schools while elevating the study of other things, is to search for a bright future in a blind alley. For humanity needs spiritual nourishment more than it needs material nourishment.

How beautiful is Mawlânâ Rûmi's saying:

Do not feed your body so much! After all, it is a sacrificial victim that will be delivered to the soil. But feed your heart as much as you can, for it is your heart that will ascend to honor. Feed the spirit with spiritual nourishment. Feed it with mature thinking, subtle understanding, and other spiritual delicacies so that it becomes powerful when it goes where it is supposed to go.

Worldly desires are like chains binding our spiritual life. If your heart is filled with self-interest, you cannot reach the presence of Allah. Inclination toward worldly desires is like a stone bound on your back: as long as it is there, you can neither swim nor fly. If a believer does not occupy himself with truth, he occupies himself with falsehood. Sa`dî of Shîrâz expressed it well: "The souls of the heedless who follow their worldly desires are disgusted with themselves."

It is a terrible confusion to look for happiness by pursuing wretched immoral actions! The goal that will guarantee our future happiness is not the attainment of some diploma handed out by mortals like ourselves, but the good pleasure of Allah the Almighty. Allah warns:

...The treasures of the heavens and the earth belong to Allah; but the hypocrites do not comprehend. (Munafiqûn, 63/7).

Let us not forget: the spirit that will give shape to societies is not the spirit of selfish pedants who memorize large numbers of books, but the spirit of those who deepen their hearts with wisdom drawn from the Qur'an and who are a source of mercy and peace for society. That is the spirit of people mindful of Allah, the faithful who love serving others.

The poet Mehmet Âkif gives the prescription that may cure the problems of humanity:

By taking inspiration directly from the Qur'an We can teach the age to understand the value of Islam...

O my Lord! May you protect us from the suffering of those unfortunates who take their wretchedness to be happiness, since they lack the true happiness that emanates from the Qur'an! May you grant us the opportunity to examine ourselves before you question us in the Hereafter and thus become servants with mature hearts! May you protect us from profligately wasting our eternal life through our transitory passions and ignorance in this world!

Amin...

CHAPTER 15

Wastefulness - 4

Concerning Morality

Our Lord commands that we organize our lives according to good moral rules, that we live with hearts sensitive to the dignity of being human. In fact, Allah the Almighty has distinguished us from other creatures through moral virtues worthy of praise, since for them, moral reflection is impossible.

A religious life without moral cultivation is unimaginable. To have faith without fortifying it with moral values is like lighting a candle in the wind without protecting it in glass. Against worldly desires and the temptations of the Devil, such unprotected faith is always in danger and at risk.

WASTEFULNESS – 4

Concerning Morality

Moral values rest on the good character traits that Allah accepts and loves to see in our actions. They are among the most precious gifts that humanity has received from Allah. In a Prophetic tradition we read, "Qualify yourselves with the qualities of Allah." (Munâwî, at-Ta`ârif, p.564). Accordingly, good character traits are dis-closures of divine attributes from the side of Beauty.

In this regard, to assume good character traits is our responsi-bility as servants, and is one of the most visible marks indicating our closeness to Allah. Good moral properties form and reveal the very dignity and integrity of human beings. That is why concern for the virtues is an attribute that singles humanity out from all creation.

The completed human being displays refined and subtle mani-festations of divine artistry in this realm of trial. Such a person stands at the peak of creation. Humanity, which is created as an exceptional alloy of unreachable heights and unfathomable depths, may preserve its high importance in the cosmos only by dedicating itself to a servanthood illuminated by moral values.

The heart is a kind of envelope where good moral properties are secured. It is created with the capacity to develop into a mirror for the divine glance. With such potentials, it is a pity if people spend their lives running after shadowy worldly desires and neglect lighting up their hearts with virtues. Such a course ends in betraying the human integrity proper for a servant of Allah. Such people lose the high position chosen for them by Reality. This means that although human beings are created in the finest manner in all creation, and Allah has assigned us a noble position, people can still act profligately and waste it all.

The aim of the science of virtue is to help us to reach our proper ideal, the perfect human being, by reminding us constantly that we are always observed by Allah and by cleansing us of immature attributes. Its aim is to plant praiseworthy properties, such as refinement, sensitivity, courtesy, generosity, modesty, and mercy, within people, so that these may grow into our fundamental nature. In this regard morality is an indispensable part of religion and faith; it is even their spirit and essence. Acknowledging this truth, our guide the Prophet ﷺ, whom Allah told us was sent to be *a mercy to worlds*, himself described his task thus: "I am sent for the perfection of character." (Muwatta, Husn al-Khulq, 8).

Thus a religious life without moral cultivation is unimaginable. To have faith without fortifying it with moral values is like lighting a candle in the wind without protecting it in glass. Against worldly desires and the temptations of the Devil, such unprotected faith is always in danger and at risk.

Good moral properties protect our religion and faith like spiritual armor. In fact, our Prophet ﷺ, the pride of the universe, declared, "Gabriel told me that Allah says: 'This religion is the religion I have chosen for Myself. For this religion, generosity and virtue are most suitable. As long as you live as Muslims, elevate religion by means of these two!" (Haythamî, VIII, 20; Ali- al-Muttaqî, *Kanz*, VI, 392).

Such is the importance of our good character to our religion. A life undirected by moral values is wasteful both of itself and of religion. But those whose hearts have a share in virtue reach the satisfaction that results from tasting the true pleasure and sweetness of faith. Here is an illustration of how good moral character serves human beings as a spiritual bridge.

There was a certain Hakîm ibn Hizâm among the Companions of the Prophet who strove for good moral qualities. He was a relative of our mother Khadîjah 🌺. Hakîm was extremely generous and compassionate, and used to love helping other people. At that time, during the Age of Ignorance, it was the custom to bury unwanted baby girls alive. Hakîm would buy such rejected daughters to protect them from their fathers.. One day he asked the Prophet 🌼, "O the Messenger of Allah! I performed good deeds in the era before Islam, such as giving charity, freeing slaves, and visiting relative. Shall I receive any reward for those actions?"

The Prophet 🌼 answered: "It is because of the good deeds you performed earlier that you have attained the honor of coming to Islam!" (Bukhârî, Zakâh, 24; Muslim, Îmân, 194-196).

There are many other examples showing the deep connection between character and faith. We might call to mind the court magicians whom Pharaoh, that claimant to divinity, brought forward to challenge Moses الله. Before that encounter, those magicians had no notion of faith in Allah. Yet they had the good fortune of a share in the secret that character is the key to faith. Indeed, they were courteous enough to offer the first move in their competition to Moses. This must have pleased Allah, for at that moment they began to incline toward that Messenger. And later on, when they saw the miraculous disclosures, these resonated with the state of their hearts, so that they were honored by faith – a faith so strong that they were ready to sacrifice their lives for it.

Pharaoh and his entourage also witnessed the miraculous acts that led the magicians to faith. Yet the same miracles led those savage folk to hold all the more tightly to their rejection of faith in Allah. In the end, the magicians were brutally killed by Pharaoh, and so reached the station of martyrdom. They also received another divine grace, for their story is related in the Qur'an and so will remain a noble memory for all believers until the Day of Judgment

Thus the spiritual benefits of moral values such as courtesy, elegance, refinement of heart, generosity and mercy are clearly visible. Good moral character is so important for divine acceptance that it helps people who display it to attain faith, the most precious of divine gifts. Imagine how the cultivation of character might help those who already have faith to climb to higher spiritual levels!

On the other hand, profligate character results in the corruption of societies and the many grave disasters that follow, culminating in massive disappointment in the Hereafter. The peaceful existence and continuity of individuals as well as societies is possible only through educating future generations with good moral character. We need descendants mindful of Allah who love their homeland and are elegant and refined of spirit. As Muhammad Iqbal stated, "Muslims are responsible for the direction the world takes."

In this regard, our Lord prohibits us from following those who fall into the madness of wastefulness by transgressing the bounds of good behavior.

And obey not the command of the prodigal, who spread corruption in the earth, and mend not (their ways). (ash-Shu'arâ, 26/151-152)

In another verse in the noble Qur'an Allah declares:

Indeed, those who love that slander should be spread concerning those who believe, theirs will be a painful punishment in this world and in the Hereafter. Allah knows. You do not know. (an-Nûr, 24/19).

Lack of modesty and good manners, which are among the most important of moral values, is the result of weakness of faith and fragile affiliation with religion. Our Prophet ﷺ underlined the relationship between moral values and faith when he said that "Modesty is part of faith." (Bukhârî, Imân, 3). Accordingly, those who encourage moral degeneration, such as the spread of immodesty and incivility in a society, commit a most loathsome crime against the faith held by that society. Certainly the common purpose of all true religions is first to establish the belief in the unity of Allah all over the world, and secondly to build a social structure shaped by good moral values.

The history of the world has witnessed many occasions when divine vengeance was activated against those who did not honor moral values but violated their boundaries. Thus history is full of lessons for those who can understand. It is sufficient education to travel the earth looking for signs to ponder. In the noble Qur'an Allah declares:

Do they not travel through the land, so that their hearts (and minds) may thus learn wisdom and their ears may thus learn to hear? Truly it is not their eyes that are blind, but the hearts that are in their breasts. (Hajj, 22/46)

When societies fall into the madness of extravagance by violating their own limits with regard to moral values, it is one of the signs indicating the coming of the Day of Judgment, which means the destruction of the whole world. That is the degree of danger attached to the waste of human character.. There are many traditions of the Prophet ﷺ telling us about the immoral acts and transgressions that will occur as the Day of Judgment approaches. Let me quote a few examples.

"There will come a time upon humanity that all people's effort and care will be directed toward their own bellies. The noble among them will be determined on the basis of wealth. Women will be their direction of prayer, and money will be their religion. Beware! These are the most dangerous of creatures. They will have no share (of the divine mercy) in the presence of Allah. (Ali al-Muttaqî, Kanzu'l-Ummâl, XI, 192/31186).

"There will come such a time upon humanity that people will not care whether they earn their livings lawfully or unlawfully." (Bukhârî, Buyû', 7).

"There will come a time upon humanity when those who tell the truth will be refuted and those who tell lies will be approved. Those who are reliable will be considered treacherous, and those who are treacherous will be held reliable. Then people will testify without being summoned, swear oaths without being asked." (Tabarânî, XXIII, 314).

"There will come such a time upon humanity that people will stop fulfilling their responsibility of enjoining the right and forbidding the wrong." (Haythamî, *Majma`az-Zawâ'id*, VII, 280). That is, they will not encourage good deeds and discourage bad deeds.

And one day, the Messenger of Allah said, "There will come a time upon humanity when the hearts of the faithful will dissolve like salt dissolves in water!"

They asked, "Why will it be so, O Messenger of Allah?"

And he replied: "It will be so, because they will not be able to eliminate the evil they encounter." (Ali a-Muttaqî, Kanz, III, 686/8463).

Abdullah ibn `Umar related the following:

The Messenger of Allah turned his face towards us and said, "O emigrants! There are five things. If you happen to like those things, I take refuge in Allah lest you attain them. They are:

1. If unlawful sexuality spreads in a society so that it is committed publicly, diseases like plague, and diseases never seen before, will spread among its people." (In my opinion, diseases like AIDS may be the realization of the warning in this tradition.)

2. "Those societies in which the scales of commerce are not kept honest will suffer famine, loss of livelihood, and injustice committed by their rulers.

3. "Those societies which refrain from paying out the share of the poor (zakâh) from their possessions shall be deprived of rain. If it were not for their animals, Allah would not give them a single drop of rain.

4. "Those societies which do not keep their promises to Allah and give up following the practice of His messenger to them shall be sent external enemies who capture their wealth.

5. "When the leaders of a society do not follow the guidance of the Qur'an but select only what they please, Allah will arrange for their punishment to arise among themselves." (Ibn Mâja, Fitan, 22; Hâkim, IV, 583/8623).

Allah the Almighty has issued many warnings in the noble Qur'an so that we may keep away from falling into such situations. He also reminded us that we are not left on our own, but are always under observation.

He utters no word but there is with him an observer ready. (Qâf, 50/18)

Thus Allah invites us to be wakeful of heart and to observe the divine limits concerning our behavior. He wishes that we refrain from extremes, from savagery, from too much and too little, from occupying ourselves with futile issues and thus squandering our lives..

Indeed there are many verses in the noble Qur'an commanding moderation in our actions and advising good moral properties. Let me cite some examples:

...And who shun vain conversation... (Mu'minûn, 23/3)

Be modest in your bearing and subdue your voice. Lo! the harshest of all voices is the voice of the ass. (Luqmân, 31 /19)

Certainly rudeness is one of the major forms of behavior that lead human beings to waste of character. Rudeness results from abandoning good moral qualities like sensitivity and courtesy. It is almost like rejecting human nature, saying farewell to what makes us human, as the example of the ass mentioned in the Qur'an would indicate.

The manner of conversation proper to human beings is, to use the Qur'anic expression, *qawl layyin*: gentle language. (Tâhâ, 20/44) Allah the Almighty commanded Moses ﷺ to use gentle language when He sent him to Pharaoh. And our Lord says:

Tell My servants to speak that which is kindlier. Indeed, the Devil sows discord among them. Indeed, the Devil is an open foe to humanity.(Isra', 17/53).

Thus Allah reminds us that we should observe the rules of courtesy when addressing other people. In another verse, Allah explains one such rule of courtesy to us, though He addresses the Prophet ﷺ :

(O Muhammad) It was by the mercy of Allah that you were lenient with them, for if you had been stern and fierce of heart, they would have dispersed from round about you. (Âl-Imrân, 3/159)

On the other hand, one must be as moderate in morality as in other affairs. Many kinds of behavior are praiseworthy when moderate, but damaging if there is either excess or shortfall in their exercise..

For example, humility is among the good moral properties. But if one is excessive in displaying humility, it becomes a sort of self-praise. This is extravagance concerning humility.

There are people who seek to convince other people of their own humbleness: ultimately the practice serves self-satisfaction. But assuming any virtue for the sake of something else is not sincere. It is hypocritical, and indeed "boasting of humility" is clearly contradictory and absurd. For example, take the following statements: "I humbly confess it takes three long days for me to recite the whole Qur'an." "Being a poor person, I was able to erect only one mosque" or "I was only able to feed such- and-such a number of people." These are all expressions displaying hypocrisy and pride under the guise of humility. Yet to humble oneself before an arrogant person and not require that a decent respect be shown, so that one falls into abasement, is another kind of waste of humility.

Both prideful distance for the sake of protecting your honor and too much casualness in human relations and friendships, especially in family life, are wastes of intimacy. Damage can result from both forms of immoderation. There is even measure to be observed in helping others. Offering too much help and too little must equally be avoided if we are to refrain from wastefulness.

The Messenger of Allah ﷺ was sensitive to issues of human dignity. He advised, "None of you should call people under your authority "my slave" or "my handmaid." All of you together are servants of Allah. Your wives also are servants of Allah. When you address the people in your family, use expressions like "my son," "my daughter" or "my brave-hearted one." (Muslim, Alfâdh, 13).

However, the Prophet ﷺ also told us also to address debauched people, who lay waste the realm of the heart and deserve divine wrath, according to their level. "Do not call a hypocrite "sir." If you take him as a gentleman, you attract the wrath of the Mighty and Majestic Lord." (Abû Dâwûd, Adab, 83; Ahmad b. Hanbal, V.346).

Thus it becomes clear that applying moral stances such as humility and courtesy in the same way in every sort of situation, without discernment, is like putting on eyeglasses without check-ing the prescription. This is extravagance in morality. Certainly, approving actions that deserve approval, disapproving actions that deserve disapproval, and treating people according to their merits is a moral requirement. The important thing is to observe the divine measure and preserve the balance of moderation in moral issues just as we are supposed to do in other issues. Only then will we be able to display the characteristics of mature believers.

Our Prophet ﷺ implemented Islamic moral values in his life with his courteous and sensitive style. Through the example of his noble personality and exquisite behavior he educated his communi-ty in many delicate points. For example, the Prophet ﷺ would never speak publicly of people's mistakes. Instead, in open gatherings he would express his critiques by saying, "What is it with me, that I see such-and-such going on?" (Bukhârî, Manâqib 25; Muslim, Salât 119). He used to frame his criticism as if there were something wrong with his sight.

Here is another example of his carefully designed method of education. One day at a feast the Prophet ﷺ noticed that someone had passed gas. He announced, "Those who have eaten camel meat should renew their ablutions!" Thus he did not single out one embarrassed person. The undesirable act became unattributable, since he technically asked all the Companions present to renew their ablution.[40]

Certainly the Prophet's own moral standards always suggested compassion, subtlety, refinement, and empathy. This is why the Messenger of Allah ﷺ was unfailingly kind to the Bedouins coming from the desert. They used to clamor at him, "Muhammad! Muhammad!" But he would answer them kindly "Please be welcome. What would you like to ask?" (Muslim, Nuzur, 8; Abû Dâwûd, Aymân, 21/3316).

Like him, we should take into account people's level of understanding when we warn them against their faults and attempt to improve them. we should also pay attention to other Prophetic examples of courtesy and rules of good manners.

It is an extremely important condition of generosity and distributing charity to observe the principles of good manners in giving. These are among the most important manifestations of good character. Indulging in regrettable actions such as reproachfully reminding other people of our help, placing them under obligation for our kindness, breaking their hearts, showing them arrogance... all this results in the loss of the reward due for good deeds and is therefore profligate. Our ancestors were quite careful about not wasting their good deeds in this way.

Our Ottoman forefathers were careful of the hearts of the mentally incompetent. It was their custom to address them by saying, "O

---

40. It is interesting that the old Zahiri legal school took this Prophetic comment to mean that eating camel meat removes ablution! It seems that those scholars did not grasp the wisdom behind the delicate approach of the Prophet.

respectable disabled one!" They did not think that such disability was a divine punishment (as was believed in Europe at the time), but viewed it as a test for able people, to see whether they would offer help. Similarly our forefathers extended a helping hand to the leprous when society pushed them out. They built a dwelling place called Miskinler Tekkesi (Lodge of the Pitiable).

They also established foundations to protect the honor of old people without relatives, since because of their modesty and dignity such people might not share their needs with others. Some foundations would provide destitute elderly women with washed and combed wool so that they could spin it and produce yarn. They would then buy back the yarn at high prices, so that the women could have the satisfaction of earning their living with their own hands.

Our forefathers also designed charity boxes for mosques that would allow people to either leave money or take it out, anonymously, so that no one would know who gave and who received.

They would deliver food to the needy in closed pots during the night, so that the feelings of the poor would not be wounded by being made identifiable to others.

Bezmialem Valide Sultan established a foundation dedicated to paying compensation for the damage caused by servants when they accidentally broke or damaged property of their master. She intended to protect the dignity of servants who were obliged to work for rude and ill-mannered people.

Indeed Allah the Almighty does not accept that His servants be humiliated. Hearts, which receive the glance of Allah, should not be hurt. Our blessed forefathers knew this very well. The courtesy, delicacy, elegance and sensitivity with which they implemented the moral principles of Islam are good examples that have gone before us.

✵

Our Lord commands that we organize our lives according to good moral rules, that we live with hearts sensitive to the dignity of being human. In fact, Allah the Almighty has distinguished us from other creatures through moral virtues worthy of praise, since for them, moral reflection is impossible.

Given this situation, to waste the distinctive quality of being human and instead live one's life in the manner of an animal, or to fall below the level of the animals, is a grave loss to the honor of humanity and a terrible madness of extravagance .

May our Lord protect us from all kinds of evil and profligacy that might lay waste our life in the Hereafter. May He grant our hearts a share of the blessing of these prayers that emerged from the gracious mouth of the Messenger of Allah: "O my Allah! May You make my inner character as beautiful as You have made my outer constitution! "O my Lord! May You lead me to attain the best of moral qualities! Certainly it is You alone who can lead me to attain them!"[41]

Amin…

---

41. Ibn Hajar, *Fath al--Bârî*, X, 456.

CHAPTER 16

Wastefulness - 5
Concerning Contemplation

True contemplation emerges at the crossroads where reason and the heart, illuminated by revelation, come together.

The Friends of Allah contemplate the works of divine art throughout the cosmos as if gazing into a deep well. They depart from there to the realms of spirit. Words fail to express the situation of a heart that feels and sees; tongues fall short of articulating it. Those who gaze upon the cosmos with such sensitivity of heart taste the joy of the wonders manifested by divine artistry.

WASTEFULNESS – 5

Concerning Contemplation

Allah the Almighty endowed humanity with special qualities like reason, logic, and the ability to reflect. He elevated humanity above all creation. The noble Qur'an explains everything by examples, and it has made clear that it only addressing rational people. Allah always asks his servants to engage in reflection, to consider all beings with an eye toward gaining wisdom, and to take lessons from them. This is why Allah invites us to contemplation in many verses in the noble Qur'an, by saying *"Do not you think?"*, *"Do not you apprehend?"*, *"…so that you may reflect,"* *"… maybe you will reflec*t," *"Take heed!"*

The noble Qur'an indicates that reason, guided by revelation, is the proper faculty for reflection, and addresses human beings with the expression "O possessors of a center!," which is interpreted by the wise as, "O people of reason!" This is why rational people who wish to pursue a life in accordance with human dignity must enter into the world of contemplation illuminated by the noble Qur'an.

We Muslim would not have hit upon many truths through reason, if Islam had not displayed before us a certain horizon of contemplation. Worse, we might have employed our reason exclusively in the pursuit of worldly desires. To protect ourselves from that disaster, we need the guidance and warnings of the noble Qur'an and the Prophetic tradition. In fact, these are the only guides that can turn human contemplation in the right direction, and that can explain the principles of living according to the straight path.

Contemplation is one of the most important acts of worship. In order to pursue a life proper to servants of Allah, we should search out the wisdom and secrets of the cosmos and study the events that occur in it. In order to achieve that goal, we must deepen our hearts through contemplation. It must be an ideal and an aspiration for every believer to reach agreement between all the thoughts in our minds and the good pleasure of Allah, between the feelings of our hearts – even the breaths we inhale or exhale – and divine acceptance. This is because Allah the Almighty created us in order to serve His grandeur. Anything that contradicts the fundamental reason for our existence falls within the definition of extravagance.

The faculty of reason, which is one of the most awesome gifts bestowed upon humanity, is not sufficient in itself to lead people to truth. The value of human contemplation depends on the harmonious functioning of both mind and heart. The mind by itself may be enough for worldly affairs and pursuit of one's own interests. But in order for us to become mature in faith, the heart, which is the center of feeling, must be educated in spiritual matters, so that it may provide guidance to reason. In fact, the heart governs reflection, and reflection governs intention. This means that the power behind all voluntary actions is the heart and the feelings rooted in it. Thus insuring that one's heart is educated according to the divine commands is more important than training all the other faculties.

The rational faculty of a person whose heart is lit up by the noble Qur'an and the Prophetic tradition acquires familiarity with the truth.

Reason and the heart are created in such a manner that they lead people to goodness and truth on the condition that they receive the light of divine guidance. True contemplation emerges at the crossroads where reason and the heart, illuminated by revelation, come together.

Attempting to puzzle out issues beyond the capacity of reason is contemplative extravagance of another sort. We are called upon to reflect on the disclosure of the divine attributes and the particularities of the noble Qur'an, the cosmos, and human beings. However, attempting to contemplate matters that are beyond human grasp, such as the divine essence or the secrets of destiny, is a waste of our mental abilities. Such attempts are prohibited by the noble Qur'an and the Prophetic tradition.

Just as there is a limit to the range of light that eyes can see, and a limit to the range of sound that ears can hear, so there is a limit to the range of truths that reason can grasp. This is why reason is in need of guidance by revelation. Just as it is a disaster not to contemplate the divine realities, so it is also a disaster if we ignore our intrinsic limitations and try to push the mind beyond its capacity. This wasteful effort is profligacy of intellect, and can result in disappointment in the Hereafter.

Human reason often operates under the influence of worldly desires and diseases of the heart such as pride and arrogance. When reason lacks the guidance of a peaceful and healthy heart, it goes astray. Contemplation undertaken in such conditions may lead to savage and perverse conclusions. Mawlânâ Jalâluddîn Rûmî said, "If Satan had had as much love as he had intellect, he would not have fallen into the situation of damnation he is in now."

Thus reason is neutral: it has no positive value on its own. It must be guided by the sensitivity originating from the heart. If the feelings occurring to our hearts can assume a spiritual character through spiritual education, then they may properly govern our reason.

Managing one's feelings is extremely difficult. However, we are obliged to work continuously to bring our feelings into accordance with the good pleasure of Allah. Our method is to engage in contemplation according to the Qur'anic precepts and the Prophetic example. Once our horizons have been expanded by such contemplative activity, by Allah's kindness and grace our thoughts and feelings will come to meet with His acceptance.

The same heart which is the abode of feelings is also the abode of faith. Indeed, faith is a noble feeling, a high sensation. Accordingly, faith is said to be the affirmation of the heart, not the affirmation of reason. The divine secrets in the cosmos can be discovered only by an intellect that operates under the guidance of a heart filled with faith. This is why the most important and the most sensitive issue concerning religion is the issue of faith. Faith does not survive when concessions made to worldly ambitions. Even a tiny crack in a glass will grow bigger and bigger, until eventually the whole glass shatters. In the realm of the heart, we must always be watchful for apparently small damages. It is necessary to head off the formation of even the smallest stain on the heart.

Reverence in worship increases the reward a servant receives for worship. Carelessness in worship decreases its reward. However, if a person reflects only upon his personal interests and a crack forms in his heart, his faith will be in danger. Carelessness in matters of faith, may Allah protect us, leads people to destruction.

There are so many cases. Qârûn makes a good example. Qârûn at first was a virtuous person. After Allah bestowed upon him a large amount of wealth, he became spoiled and arrogant. He began to feel that he had accumulated his wealth entirely by his own efforts. He became so proud and blind that he attempted to oppose the Prophet Moses ﷺ. Finally Allah the Almighty buried him underground, with all his wealth. In the noble Qur'an his end is described in the following manner:

So We caused the earth to swallow him and his dwelling-place. Then he had no host to help him against Allah, nor was he of those who can save themselves. (Qasas, 28/81)

A heart that loses its grounding in faith is like a knife that slips while one is cutting bread: just a moment of negligence and there is injury. The knife slips in an instant, and our feelings manifest in an instant.

The heart where feelings emerge is the freest organ in the body. Its inclinations can shift at any time. The Prophet ﷺ said, "The heart is between the two fingers of the All-Compassionate, and He turns it howsoever He pleases." The heart has a share of the divine attribute the Guider, and also a share of the divine attribute the Misguider. No one knows when either of them may dominate the other.

Another example is Bal`am ibn Bawrah, whose story is mentioned in the noble Qur'an. His inclination toward the worldly cravings originating from his lower soul destroyed him. At first he was among the virtuous servants of Allah. He even manifested miracles, and his prayers were granted. But ultimately he inclined toward his selfish desires: he entrusted the control of his reason to his ego, and this resulted in his destruction. The noble Qur'an tells his story as following:

Recite unto them the tale of him to whom We gave Our revelations, but he sloughed them off, so Satan overtook him and he became of those who lead astray. And had We willed We could have raised him by their means, but he clung to the earth and followed his own lust. Therefore his likeness is as the likeness of a dog: if you attack him he pants with his tongue out, and if you leave him alone he pants with his tongue out. Such is the likeness of the people who deny Our revelations. Narrate unto them the history (of the people of old), that haply they may take thought. (A'râf, 7/175).

As I have explained above, attempting to use reason outside the control of revelation and for the sake of realizing selfish desires makes human beings stupid, and leads them into the kind of confusion mentioned in the preceding Qur'anic verse. This is why the Prophet ﷺ used to pray saying: "O my Lord! May you not leave me to my self even if it is only for the blink of an eye."[42] This saying displays the spiritual state of the ideal believer.

Thus in order to save our faith, we must undergo an education of feeling that keeps us poised between fear and hope, and directs our contemplation accordingly. If we aim to die with believing hearts, we must keep our hearts sensitive and aware throughout our lives. Indeed Allah the Almighty states in the noble Qur'an:

O you who believe! Observe your duty to Allah with right observance, and die not except in a state of Islam. (Âl-Imrân, 3/102).

For example, if we do not love and hate for the sake of Allah, we will love that which we should hate and hate that which we should love, and spiritual disaster will ensue. One must learn to direct both love and hate where they belong. The company of servants who are mindful of Allah draws a believer into happiness. In the noble Qur'an Allah declares:

O you who believe! Be careful of your duty to Allah, and be with the truthful. (at-Tawbah, 9/119).

42. *Jâmi` as-Saghîr*, v. I, p. 58

On the other hand, to attach oneself to an enemy of religion is a prelude to disaster. In this regard, Allah says:

...sit not, after your remembrance, in the congregation of evildoers. (An'âm, 6/68).

Thus in order to engage in sound contemplation, our feelings must be illuminated by light from the divine source.

In a different verse in the noble Qur'an, Allah declares:

Lo! We offered the trust unto the heavens and the earth and the mountains, but they shrank from bearing it and were afraid of it. And the human being assumed it, who has been a tyrant and a fool. (Ahzâb, 33/72).

Since humanity has not been able properly to appreciate the weight of the trust we assumed, in this verse we are characterized as *zalûm* (tyrannical) and *jahûl* (violently ignorant). These expressions are meant to underline the importance of the trust and to call people to pay attention. In order to get rid of the characteristics *zalûm* and *jahûl,* we must do praiseworthy deeds and be able to turn our inner and outer knowledge into direct recognition of the presence of Allah via contemplation. In this regard, our Lord informs us n the Qur'anic chapter `Asr that in order for humanity to free itself from disappointment we must have faith, do praiseworthy deeds, and advise each other toward truth and forbearance – which is an act of worship that results from serving the wellbeing of the whole community. Pointing out the depth and density of meaning in the verses of this chapter, Imam Shafi'î remarked, "If people were to reflect upon Surah `Asr and analyze it properly, it would suffice for them." (Ibn Kathîr, *Commentary on Surah `Asr*).

In the noble Qur'an, our Lord opens for us a wide horizon of contemplation. One of the verses that must be considered in this regard is the following:

They remember Allah standing, sitting, and lying on their sides, and reflect upon the creation of the heavens and the earth, (saying): Our Lord! You did not create this in vain. Glory be to You! So preserve us from the suffering of the Fire. (Âl-Imrân, 3/191)

The beautiful manifestations of divine power in the realm of space (such as the wonders manifest in the earth and the heavens) and the realm of time (such as the changes related to night and day) –all these invite people of reflective intelligence to draw closer to Allah. Allah the Almighty wishes us to be acquainted with the cosmic language. Indeed all beings speak to those who are available for the divine illuminations. All things, from atoms to the planet, can remind humanity of the glory of our Lord.

When servants contemplate the disclosures of divine glory in the cosmos, we are led to humility and finally to the realization of our nothingness. The maturity of a believer rests upon his comprehension of the fact that he is weak and limited before his Lord. Only the acceptance of the fact of our smallness and incapacity in the face of the grandeur and immensity of Allah can do away with the rampant diseases of pride and self-admiration.

In this regard the Prophet ﷺ used to pray, asking Allah for forgiveness, "O my Lord! We are not able to know You as You should be known..." (Munâwî II, 520).

The ego of anyone who has never tasted impotence and despair is like a wild stallion. Pharaoh, Nimrod (persecutor of Abraham), Qârûn, and Haman were all like this. Such people enjoy the suffering of others. For them, the cries of the afflicted are like pleasant melodies.

On the other hand if a person suffers some disease, disaster, or tragedy in the world, but is able to take heed of it, the pain he has lived through will turn out to be good for him. This is because the experience of inability, despair, and nothingness leads such a person in the direction of modesty and humility, and causes him to cry "O my Allah!" from the depths of his heart.

Again, people reach levels of maturity that are commensurate to the sufferings they undergo and the difficulties they overcome. This is why Allah the Exalted made His prophets and virtuous servants subject to ordeals according to their various spiritual levels. Such ordeals turned out to be manifestations of divine grace, and served the perfection of their spiritual status.

Sheikh Sâ`dî of Shirâz declared, "For those who reflect, every leaf of every tree, no matter how thin it may be, is like a thick detailed book providing knowledge of Allah (that is, the heart's recognition of Allah). For rough fools, all the trees on earth do not amount to a single leaf."

In order for our sense-organs and intellect to be able to perceive the divine secrets in the universe, our reason must be shaped by contemplation and our heart must have spiritual depth. The course of divine power through the cosmos is like soundless and wordless divine poetry. This divine poetry gains profundity only insofar as the heart perceives it.

The Friends of Allah contemplate the works of divine art throughout the cosmos as if gazing into a deep well. They depart from there to the realms of spirit. Words fail to express the situation of a heart that feels and sees; tongues fall short of articulating it. Those who gaze upon the cosmos with such sensitivity of heart taste the joy of the wonders manifested by divine artistry.

Such people turn their attention to the marvelously diverse leaves and flowers of plants, which all grow out of the same soil; upon their fruits that differ in terms of color, smell, taste and form. They look at the butterfly, displaying extraordinary patterns in its wings despite a lifespan of only two weeks. They listen to the secret messages that all things announce in the language of their natures. For such people, the universe is a book waiting to be read.

Meanwhile, ignorant people in whom the seas of intellect and heart run shallow or dry watch only the outer covering of things. They remain unaware of the spiritual pearls within. Mawlânâ Jalâluddîn Rûmî describes them:

Those whose hearts are filled with the love of the world are like hunters of shadows. How can anyone possess a shadow? Indeed, a foolish hunter took the shadow of a bird to be the bird itself, and attempted to catch it. Even the bird perched on the branch of the tree was amazed by the action of this foolish hunter!

A Friend of Allah stated, "For the intelligent, this life consists of watching divine beauties. For the foolish, it consists of satisfying selfish desires."

The people of heart consider this world with the intention of taking heed and learning the wisdom behind all things. They recognize a subtle disclosure in everything, and so obtain wise insights from the world. Those who are ignorant say, "Take it easy, and try your best to enjoy whatever you can: we come to this world but once!" Such an attitude increases the darkness and fragmentation of their hearts.

Mawlânâ Jalâluddîn Rûmî invites us to come to our senses, think about our situation, and consider the wisdom behind our existence in the universe.

Observe the human community wisely! ... Why do you consider your bodily desires and individual interests as important as great mountains? And why do you consider a man with sound contemplation as unimportant as an ant? Why are you blind and foolish, although you see the course of divine greatness and power running through the universe? O you who fall *lowest of the low*! Just as a stone knows nothing, you know nothing of contemplation. How unfortunate you are! Since you have lost contemplation, you are deprived of the greatest bliss.

It is very sad when the divine bounty of contemplation is subjugated to selfish desires. To live without reflection is a sign of laziness and rough ignorance. To lose one's sensitivity is to let one's heart go blind and deaf, and for the heart to remain indifferent before all these divine disclosures is not compatible with human dignity. There is no question about it: to stare uncomprehendingly at the cosmos with stupid and glowering looks is a spiritual disaster. This situation is described In the Qur'an:

(O My Messenger!) Do they (those who oppose you) not travel through the land, so that their hearts (and minds) may thus learn wisdom and their ears may thus learn to hear? Truly it is not their eyes that are blind, but the hearts that are in their breasts. (Hajj, 22/46)

Mawlânâ considers using the faculty of reflection improperly to be like "putting trash in a golden bowl." That is a perfect image for wasting the bounties of contemplation and awareness by using them for sake of mundane and base desires.

One must practice reflection properly, and in a proper environment. Otherwise, thinking goes off course, and may lead the unwise to spiritual disappointment. Those who do not take the divine warnings into account shall be regretful in the Hereafter for wasting the divine bounty of contemplation by directing it toward the satisfaction of their selfish desires. The noble Qur'an explains this :

Therein will they cry aloud (for assistance): "Our Lord! Bring us out: we shall work righteousness, not the (deeds) we used to do!" "Did We not give you long enough life so that he who would, should receive admonition? And (moreover) the warner came to you. So taste you (the fruits of your deeds): for wrongdoers there is no helper. (Fatir 35/37).

Thus we must use our reason properly in order to reach salvation in the Hereafter. We must illuminate our feelings and thoughts with light from the divine source, not with grandiose satanic suggestions or selfish desires. Mawlânâ states that one must be very careful in this regard. "The devilish thoughts, imaginations and misgivings that emerge in us are like thorns in our hearts. These thorns come not only from one single person, but from thousands of people, and pierce into our hearts."

We must protect ourselves from misgivings that originate in our animal souls or in the Devil, since these destroy the spiritual attunement of our hearts and ruin our faculties of contemplation and sensitivity. A radio tuned to the wrong channel cannot receive the transmissions of another broadcasting station, and so it is with the heart. If it remains in misapprehension and ignorance, it will pick up no guidance and its destination is destruction. Fish live best in the sea, and creatures of land live best on the earth. Similarly, the human soul reaches happiness within the illuminated climate of the noble Qur'an and the Prophetic tradition.

The most important horizon of contemplation is certainly contemplation of death. It saves us from the deception of devilish temptations and intoxication with bodily pleasures, and so makes a human being the possessor of a cognizant heart. In the noble Qur'an, Allah says:

And the stupor of death comes to him. (And it is announced to him:) "This is the thing which you were trying to escape!" (Qâf, 50/19).

In a tradition, the Prophet ﷺ declares: "Remember death as much as possible, since it destroys the pleasures." (Tirmidhî, Qiyâmah 26).

Mature people are those who decode the hints concerning life after death and get ready for the next life while they live this one. Unless one contemplates life after death, one cannot know the secrets of our common future. It is necessary for anyone who has a sound intellect to reflect properly, in a climate of awareness and attention, upon the meaning of our short journey between the cradle and the grave.

To untie the knot concerning the future is not possible through simple human reflection. One can achieve this only if one submits oneself to the guidance of revelation. Otherwise we will merely exhaust ourselves in the vain attempt to escape from death.

Allah the Almighty invites us to His Paradise. That is why He warns us against heedlessness. In the noble Qur'an, Allah says:

Did you then think that We had created you in vain, and that you would not be brought back to Us (for accounting)? (Mu'minûn, 23/115)

In this regard, the Prophet ﷺ asked Allah for protection from losing our contemplation and sensitivity under the intrusion of worldly affaires, and prayed, "O my Allah! May You not make the world our greatest thought and purpose, and the peak to which our knowledge can reach!..." (Tirmidhî, Da'awât, 79).

Again our Prophet ﷺ invited us to contemplation even through the prayers he offered before going to sleep. Through his own example, he commended a gratitude and glorification that are simultaneous with a keen awareness of the state of the poor: "Praise belongs to Allah who feeds us and quenches our thirst, who protects and shelters us, for how many there are who have no protection or shelter" (Muslim, Dhikr, 6). It is a significant responsibility of the servants of Allah to contemplate the divine bounties received during each day and to thank Allah the Almighty for them. One must think about the importance of being able to get into bed with a full belly while so many people in the world fall asleep without food and water; to lie down to sleep with a feeling of satisfaction and security, while so many people are subject to poverty and danger; and to rest comfortably, while so many people spend the night without a roof over their heads because of disasters that have fallen upon them.

Great bounties mean great responsibilities. Thus making a reckoning of what we have received each day before going to bed that night has an indispensable place in the life of contemplation. Indeed `Umar, the second caliph ﷺ who said, "Reckon up your soul before the accounting is required of you," used to painstakingly evaluate his conscience. He took his position as leader extremely seriously. "If a sheep should drown in the Tigris," he once remarked, "Allah will question `Umar about it." And he would address himself, "Umar, what have you done today for Allah?"

How many times, I wonder, have we experienced such feelings? We tire ourselves out in pursuit of a livelihood, but how many nights have we subjected our hearts to a reckoning? How much time do we spend thinking about why we are created, where we have come from and where we are going, and to what extent our lives are acceptable to Allah? How much time do we devote to examining how fully we have implemented the requirements of our religion? To what extent do we shape our lives according to the commands of our Lord? How deep can we go into the cultural and spiritual world of the noble Qur'an, which is Allah's message communicated to us? And how far might we imitate the beautiful examples in the life of the Prophet ﷺ, whose life was the animate Qur'an? How much do we care about our shortcomings in these matters? Or have we lost our best treasury of contemplation?

The Qur'an relates to us the story of Habîb an-Najjâr, who suffered stoning by the members of his tribe but saved his faith; the story of the people of Uhdûd who were burnt in ditches; and the story of the magicians who were subject to Pharaoh's torture after they reached the guidance of Allah. We are given all these exemplary cases. But how much are we aware of the value of Allah's gift, our faith?

May Allah the Almighty keep us away from being deprived of contemplation, as well as from becoming wasteful of this great divine bounty! May he make our hearts, minds, and senses follow a course suitable to His divine approval!

Amin...

CHAPTER 17

Wastefulness - 6

Concerning Livelihood and Charity

It is well known that the causes behind the spiritual crisis of our time are unlawful earnings, violation of the rights of others, lack of contentment with one's possessions, and the craving for earning more. In order to eliminate these negative motives, people must be mindful of the Islamic principles warning us against infringing the rights of others and encouraging us to earn our livelihood in lawful ways.

❊

In any society there will be people who may be doing less than their opportunities would oblige them to do. If we compare our own actions to the actions of such people and consider ourselves generous by comparison, that comparison may not be sound. This is why we should compare our own level of generosity to the practice of the Prophet ﷺ and his Companions.

WASTEFULNESS – 6

Concerning Livelihood and Charity

This worldly life, our test, is embellished with innumerable divine bounties, disclosures to the wise of the power and greatness of Allah the Almighty. These bounties may inspire people to become better servants. They may also produce discord and disappointment, if servants remain negligent. It would be utterly profligate to waste the bounties entrusted to us by Allah by using them contrary to their proper aim, or for the sake of selfish desires and devilish ambitions.

Certainly Allah the Almighty put all things between the heavens and the earth under the dominion of humanity. But he also told us that people shall be held responsible for these bounties in the Hereafter. Indeed, Allah tells us in the noble Qur'an:

Then, shall you be questioned that Day about the profits (you took!). (at-Takâthur, 102/8)

You shall certainly be tried and tested in your possessions and in your personal selves… (Âl-Imrân, 3/186)

Did you then think that We had created you in vain, and that you would not be brought back to Us (for accounting)? (Mu'minûn, 23/115)

The most upsetting kind of profligacy (which means wasteful-ness and violation of rightful limits) is the one that results from transgressing the boundaries set by Allah, and thus exchanging eternal happiness in the Hereafter for disappointment.

Out of ignorance, people usually think that wastefulness only concerns excessive consumption of material goods, and thus they apply the concept only within a narrow framework. However, just as wastefulness in the disposal of material goods is forbidden, so wastefulness in the disposal of spiritual goods is forbidden as well. Furthermore, profligacy concerning spiritual goods brings heavier responsibilities and may lead to disappointment.

Among the most important areas in which people behave wastefully both materially and spiritually are those that occur in the course of daily earning, spending, and charity.

Allah has determined the sustenance of all His servants. In fact, in the Qur'an Allah explains that the sustenance of people is guaranteed:

I have only created jinn and men so that they may serve Me. No sustenance do I require of them, nor do I require that they should feed Me. For Allah is He Who gives (all) Sustenance, Lord of Power, Steadfast (for ever). (Zâriyât, 51/56-58)

How many are the creatures that carry not their own sustenance? It is Allah who feeds (both) them and you: for He hears and knows (all things). (`Ankabût, 29/60)

There is no moving creature on earth but its sustenance depends on Allah: He knows the time and place of its definite abode and its temporary placement. All is in a clear record. (Hûd, 11/6)

In these verses Allah the Almighty assures us that His knowl-edge, power, and mercy are infinite. Indeed, we are unable even to imagine the number of animals living under the darkness of the soil, in hidden corridors of the earth, and deep down in the oceans. But Allah's knowledge comprehends everything concerning them and guarantees their food and livelihood. So while we seek after our own sustenance, we must contemplate how we might establish companionship of heart with the ultimate Provider: Allah the Almighty, who provides sustenance for all.

The fact that Allah the Almighty guarantees the sustenance of creatures is an indication of divine power. This is stated elegantly in a saying of the Prophet ﷺ : "Don't give up your hopes of sustenance as long as you can lift your head. For man is born from his mother naked, and scarlet from head to toe. Afterwards Allah, the mighty and exalted, provides a wide range of sustenance for him." (Ibn Mâja, Zuhd, 14). He also said, "Allah is very rich. What human beings eat and drink subtracts nothing from his wealth. He is very generous, and bestows His bounties endlessly, day and night. Think what Allah has bestowed upon creatures since the creation of the heavens and the earth! None of it has decreased His wealth." (Bukhârî, Tawhid, 22).

Knowing this, if we worry too much about obtaining our sustenance and exaggerate our efforts in that regard, we are only allowing free sway to an anxiety originating from our lower soul, and one must keep clear of such anxieties. Only in relevant ways and through lawful means should we try our best to obtain the sustenance allotted us by Allah. We must consider the results of our lawful efforts as the decision of Allah, recognize them to be what is best for us, and accept them. If we succumb to unreasonable worries regarding the acquisition of sustenance and forget the Provider, of if we pursue unlawful means in order to gain more than we have, we are transgressing the limits and falling into profligacy.

At the same time, we must beware assuming that since Allah has decreed our sustenance from eternity, we are not in need of making any efforts. Such pernicious thinking that urges people to laziness also issues from the narrow focus of the lower soul. Such thinking, in trying to keep away from unreasonable worry, only passes to the other extreme

Allah the Almighty describes the situation in the Hereafter of those who transgress the divinely set limits through greed and avarice, and devote themselves to loving the wealth of this world.

Who piled up wealth and laid it by, thinking that his wealth would make him last forever? By no means! He will be sure to be thrown into That which Breaks to Pieces. And what will explain to you That which Breaks to Pieces? (It is) the Fire of (the wrath of) Allah kindled (to a blaze), which leaps up to the hearts. It shall close in on them, as if they were bound to outstretched columns. (Humazah 104/2-9)

The Messenger of Allah ﷺ expressed concern that his community might fall into extravagance by abandoning proper behavior in the pursuit of wealth. He said, "I fear that after I leave you, you will be presented with the flowers (goods) and ornaments of the world (and you may fall in love with them)!" (Bukhârî, Zakâh, 47)

It is not acceptable for us to become so occupied with earning our livelihood that we neglect private prayers and community services. It is also not acceptable to go to the other extreme and become indifferent and lazy concerning the livelihood of our families, so that they are in danger of falling into deprivation and ruin. The acceptable and blessed way, free from extravagance, is one that does not drive people to neglect performance of their ritual acts, nor damages anyone's wellbeing, but provides a balanced order of work leading to lawful sustenance that brings happiness to the family.

On the other hand, it is worth pursuing the wealth of this world in order to give charity to the weak, those who live unprotected and under poor conditions. The possessor of such wealth may reach inner peace and the happiness of the Hereafter, for generosity and mercy belong among the character traits of the faithful.

Mercy is the most precious fruit of faith. Mercy is manifested most clearly when we try our best, using all lawful means, to help people in need recover from deprivation. We pass the bounties bestowed upon us by Allah along to the needy as charity.

How beautiful is the expression of Mawlânâ! "This worldly life is a dream. To become rich in this world is like finding a treasure in a dream. The wealth of this world remains in it, transmitted from one generation to the other."

If we leave all our wealth to our heirs and descendants, we do not know what will become of it. They may lack proper spiritual training, and we cannot guess how they will spend their inheritance. Accumulating family wealth means assuming a heavy responsibility in the Hereafter. Such an undertaking may be unwise, for sound reasons. The Qur'an warns:

...And there are those who bury gold and silver and spend it not in the way of Allah. Announce unto them a most grievous penalty. (at-Tawbah, 9/34)

Our Prophet ﷺ one day asked his Companions: "Which of you loves the wealth of his heirs more than his own wealth?"

His Companions replied, "O Messenger of Allah! We all love our own wealth more than the wealth of our heirs!"

Then the Prophet ﷺ said, "Whatever a person sends ahead of him to the Hereafter, by spending it on charity, is his own (true) wealth. Whatever he doesn't spend is left behind and becomes the wealth of his heirs!" (Bukhârî, Riqâq 12)

Shaykh Sa'dî gave the following advice regarding the proper management of riches. "Don't think that by piling up money, your status will rise! Water that doesn't flow, stinks. Try to forgive and give charity. The heavens open to help the flowing water; by rains and by floods they support it. Intelligent people take their property with them when they depart to the other world. (That is, they give it as charity when they are alive to obtain divine acceptance). It is only miserly people who miss their property so much that they leave it behind them here!"

Abû Hurayrah ﷺ related that a man came to the Prophet ﷺ and asked him, "O Messenger of Allah! Which alms will earn the most reward?"

Our Prophet ﷺ replied, "The greatest reward belongs to the alms given when you are strong, powerful, healthy, and have some wish to hold on to them, since you are either afraid of becoming poor or desirous of becoming wealthy. Don't postpone giving alms until you feel close to death, and then start saying, 'This much shall be given to so-and-so, and that much shall be given to so-and-so! 'Indeed at that moment your property has already been claimed by your inheritors." (Bukhârî, Zakâh 11)

Abdullah ibn Shihhîr ﷺ related: "One day the Messenger of Allah was reciting the Qur'anic chapter at-Takâthur. When he completed his recitation, he said: "The children of Adam keep saying, 'My property, my property!' O children of Adam! Do you have any property other than what you have consumed by eating it and wearing it, or by sending it to the Hereafter in advance by giving it as charity, so that you may be rewarded for it there?" (Muslim, Zuhd, 3-4).

Again, the Messenger of Allah ﷺ said, "If one of you reaches the morning with life and possessions so secure that you have your health and a daily meal, you are like someone to whom the whole world has been given." (Tirmidhî, Zuhd, 34)

And, "How happy is the one who was led to the straight path of Islam, who has sufficient livelihood and is satisfied with what he has!" (Tirmidhî, Zuhd, 35)

And, "A person who surrenders to Allah, has a bare livelihood, and is thankful has certainly attained salvation." (Muslim, Zakâh, 125)

Abû Umâmah ʿIyâs ibn Thaʾlabah ﷺ said, "Once, in the Prophet's presence, his Companions were talking about worldly affairs. The Messenger of Allah remarked, "Don't you hear, don't you hear? Pursuing a simple life is part of having faith! Pursuing a simple life is part of having faith!." (Abû Dâwûd, Tarajjul, 2)

Indeed, recalling Thaʾlabah provides an occasion for mature believers to take heed. He began as virtuous man, but was caught up in the craving for worldly wealth. He did not pay attention to the warnings and guidance of the Prophet, and finally ended sadly through the intoxication of wealth.

Our Prophet ﷺ declared, "The son of Adam may lay claim to nothing but a house to inhabit, a cloth to cover his body, a piece of bread to eat, and a cup of water." (Tirmidhî, Zuhd, 30)

The Messenger of Allah advised the faithful to pursue a life without waste, to be content with what they had, and to be moderate. He lived in this way himself, as an example to his community. His mode of life is reflected in this prayer of his: "O my Lord! May you provide as sustenance to the family of Muhammad exactly what will suffice." (Bukhârî, Riqâq, 17)

It is well known that the causes behind the spiritual crisis of our time are unlawful earnings, violation of the rights of others, lack of contentment with one's possessions, and the craving for earning more. In order to eliminate these negative motives, people must be mindful of the Islamic principles warning us against infringing the rights of others and encouraging us to earn our livelihood in lawful ways.

Certainly, whether your wealth is earned lawfully or unlawfully affects your dealings with Allah and your dealings with others. Therefore it affects your fate. Lawful or unlawful income is also frequently found to be the issue underpinning either the positive or the negative behavior of our children. If we want ideal children free from negative and base influences, we must make sure that our wealth is earned lawfully.

If hearts constantly observe Allah's commands and the tradition of the Messenger, they will demand lawful sustenance, and bodies nourished on such sustenance become a source of light and goodness. As for bodies that are polluted by unlawful food or food of doubtful origins, they will become a source of evil. Consequently, those who love the Prophet ﷺ will follow his advice. They will keep away from extravagance as well as miserliness and will be careful to earn their sustenance by lawful means. Following the Prophet's illumined path, they will enjoy the happiness of keeping company with him in the Hereafter.

Be aware that needs and requirements differ from one age to another. Needs should be satisfied according to their level of urgency. If we are giving money and effort in charity but not satisfying actual needs, such actions are classified as a kind of wastefulness, merely because of our failure to estimate true needs. For example, when a society badly needs educated people of faith with a sense of dignity, people who love their fellow Muslims, if we spend our charity elsewhere, we are wasting it. In a period when implementation of religious principle and development of spiritual feeling alike are weakening, the most urgent need is to support them and make an effort to increase the level of religious, moral, and spiritual education.

Believers must develop their ability to identify need. Allah the Exalted explains the importance of making sure that charity is given to the neediest Thus He says in the noble Qur'an:

(Charity is) for those in need, who, in Allah's cause, are restricted (from travel), and cannot move about in the land, seeking (for trade or work). The ignorant man thinks, because of their modesty, that they are free from want. You shall know them by their faces... (Baqarah, 2/73)

While there are so many people who are needy, it is immoderate to give people we know personally more than they require. That is, we must give charity to the needy strictly according to their need.

Mawlânâ Jalâluddîn Rûmî remarked:

There are many wealthy men who, if they were to refrain from giving charity to the undeserving, would profit more from their restraint than they do from their charity. Spend the property bestowed by Allah upon you according to the divine rules! Giving charity without proper grounds makes you into a rebellious slave who gives the king's property to bandits while pretending to be generous.

Those who are in charge of maintaining humanitarian foundations and associations must be particularly aware of this principle and extremely careful when they deliver charity to the needy.

There is another important point to which we should pay attention. A certain behavior undertaken in different circumstances may appear to be the same both times, yet it will be counted differently according to the situation. While certain acts may be counted as profligate when performed by one person, the same acts may be counted otherwise when performed by another person, for people have different opportunities regarding both the spiritual and the material bounties they possess. Consequently, the responsibility of each person to Allah depends on that person's capacities. In the noble Qur'an, Allah declares:

On no soul does Allah place a burden greater than it can bear... (Baqarah, 2/286).

So we see that according to the divine measurement, no person's responsibility is equal to anyone else's.

A developed human being should give the greatest amount of charity possible according to his or her opportunity and possession. Certainly we are all are under obligation, and will be held responsible for the good works that we might have done, yet held back from doing.

Still, in any society there will be people who may be doing less than their opportunities would oblige them to do. If we compare our own actions to the actions of such people and consider ourselves generous by comparison, that comparison may not be sound. This is why we should compare our own level of generosity to the practice of the Prophet ﷺ and his Companions. We should make their behavior our criteria for assessing acts of charity, and try to imitate them. Those who appear generous in the eyes of men may not be so in the eyes of Allah.

May Allah the Almighty lead us to refrain from the unlawful and suspect in all affairs! May He preserve our hearts from inclining toward either extravagance or miserliness! May He grant that we use all His bounties in accordance with His consent, and let us come into His presence with shining faces and peace of mind!

Amin…

CHAPTER 18

Wastefulness - 7
Concerning Health and the Consumption
of Food and Drink

One feels terribly shaken when one sees the wastefulness dominating our habits of consumption of food and drink, in our daily life and especially during wedding ceremonies and feasts. Preparing ostentatious banquets to show off pride and power, encouraging gluttony with all-you-can-eat meals, strutting about foolishly in expensive designer clothes – all these excessive behaviors will certainly bring regret in the Hereafter, since we shall be questioned on these expenditures according to the divine measure.

WASTEFULNESS– 7

Concerning Health and the Consumption of Food and Drink

Health is one of the underappreciated divine bounties. Our Prophet ﷺ warns of the common ignorance and negligence in this regard. "There are two divine blessings that people do not properly value," he said, "health and leisure." (Bukhârî, Riqâq, 1). Thus he warns us, his community, against the remorse we may suffer for wasting these two precious gifts.

Ibn ʿUmar ﷺ reported that the Messenger of Allah said, "When you reach the morning, don't wait for the evening. When you reach the evening, don't wait for the morning. When you are healthy, take precautions for the time when you may be sick. Throughout you life, take precautions for the time you die." (Bukhârî, Riqâq, 3)

Allah entrusted each of us with a body, and our bodies have due rights over us. In fact, in order to pursue the life of servanthood properly, it is necessary to maintain physical as well as spiritual health. Acts of worship may only be performed fully when a person has a healthy body. Is it possible for someone who is not healthy to offer ritual prayers serenely or to fast with inner peace? So many ritual acts and good works that allow people's hearts to draw closer to Allah depend on the blessing of health. When one loses one's health, one's acts of worship and of service lose their wholeness. Thus when we still have the opportunity to keep ourselves healthy, we should thank Allah properly for this bounty and pay close attention to our worship and the giving of charity.

Just as with all other bounties, health may be wasted if one does not follow the divine instructions concerning its preservation. Smoking may not be considered very important, but one can lose one's health by it, as one can by indulging in various forbidden acts. To throw your health away is to treat your body profligately. In order to avoid wasting our health, we must protect it by following the guidance of reason and the divine commands. This involves seeking healthy nourishment, but also protecting our bodies from natural factors like excessive heat and cold, and from the results of negligence, such as traffic accidents.

Our religion includes a variety of material and spiritual teachings concerning the protection of health. It orders us to be prudent in the consumption of food. It advises that we should not go to places where a contagious disease has been identified, but that if we have contracted a contagious disease, we should not travel from where we are. It provides basic principles of preventive medicine through an array of commands and counsels.

Our religion informs us that in order to protect our health, spiritual precautions are also necessary. These include being careful to pay the share of the poor out of our wealth, and giving alms. The Messenger of Allah ﷺ indicated the extent of spiritual precautions needed protect health. He said, "An act of charity is due for every joint of the human body. This is why every instance of declaring Allah's glory counts as charity; every instance of thanking Allah counts as charity, every recitation of "There is no god but Allah" counts as charity; every declaration of" Allah is greater" counts as charity; to give good advice is charity; to warn against something evil is charity. The ritual prayer of two cycles performed before noon has the same status." (Bukhârî, Sulh, 11).

Certainly being healthy and happy are great blessings that oblige their possessor to thank Allah. This obligation may be satisfied by giving alms out of one's material goods. It may also be satisfied by the recitation of litanies, by performing ritual worship, and by a variety of actions undertaken to serve others so that one may please Allah.

The respected Companions of the Prophet, who are presented to us as role models because of their high virtues,[43] made great efforts in the cause of Allah because they took the bounties bestowed by Allah as capital to invest toward the life of the Hereafter. Allah the Almighty blessed their efforts. The modern lifestyle, with its overconsumption, gluttony, luxury and ostentation, was not practiced by the Companions of the Prophet. They pursued their lives in accordance with their consciousness that "the soul's mansion tomorrow will be the grave."

If the body, which is entrusted to us for a certain period, is not properly fed, whether because of miserliness or for some other reason, it will be subject to various kinds of weakness and diseases. Overfeeding it will produce a similar result. Whether one overfeeds it on lawful or unlawful food, there will be physical illness. However, if the body is fed on unlawfully obtained food, in addition to losing our bodily health, we may lose our spiritual health as well.

The higher a person's spiritual state, the greater care that person takes concerning food and drink. For example, according to the religious law, to keep eating after one's hunger is satisfied

---

43. See at-Tawbah, 9/100.

is accounted wasteful. According to the Sufi path, to keep eating *until* one's hunger is satisfied is accounted wasteful. At the level of truth, to eat without remembering the divine presence is accounted wasteful. And at the level of recognition of Allah, to eat without contemplating the divine disclosure manifested in the gift of food is accounted wasteful.

The hidden guide Khidr 🕮 visited `Abdulkhâliq Gujduwânî 🕮, one of the Friends of Allah. The conversation between the two concerning the consumption of food and drink is full of lessons, since it displays the peak of spiritual sensitivity.

Showing hospitality, `Abdulkhâliq Gujduwânî offered Kidr food, but Khidr 🕮 refused to eat it, and moved away from the table. `Abdulkhâliq Gujduwânî was surprised. "This is a lawfully obtained food," he said." Why don't you eat?"

Khidr replied, "Yes, it is obtained lawfully, but the one who prepared it cooked it with anger and in heedlessness."

Thus the spiritual quality of our food is influenced not only by whether the food was lawfully obtained, but also by the psychological condition of whoever prepares it. And the spiritual qualify of our inner attitudes and ritual acts is influenced by the quality of our food. So look at how sensitive we must be concerning the food that we eat.

Food sold through public display is set before the eyes of people, some of whom are likely to be poor people who desire to have it but cannot afford it. These people have a certain right over such food because of having been exposed to it. Also, we do not know how commercial foods are prepared. Unfortunately, people are frequently careless about the harm that such foods may cause.

However, the history of the food we consume, that is, the way it was made and comes to us, influences our state.

Lawfully obtained food has an important part in purifying the heart. Abdulqâdir Gaylânî ﷺ stated, "Eating unlawfully obtained food kills the heart; eating lawfully obtained food enlivens it. There is food that makes you occupied with the world. There is also food that makes you occupied with the Hereafter. There is even food that makes you love Allah the Exalted."

Mawlânâ Jalâladdîn Rûmî ﷺ said, "Last night some doubtful bits of food went down to my stomach and closed the way by which inspiration comes." His statement shows that we must be as careful about the spiritual quality of the food we consume as we are about its material quality.

Mawlânâ also said, "Do not feed your body so much! After all, it is a sacrificial victim that will be delivered to the soil. But feed your heart as much as you can, for it is your heart that will ascend to honor. ...Feed your body less, because those who feed it more than is necessary begin pursuing selfish desires, and are destined to disgrace."

To act immoderately in such matters is not suitable to the dignity of a believer.

Our virtuous predecessors said, "Allah summarized the entire science of medicine in a half verse of the Qur'an:

...Eat and drink, but do not waste by excess!... (A'raf, 7/31).

They emphasized the importance of keeping away from waste when consuming food and drink so that one might have a healthy life in spiritual as well as material terms.[44]

---

44. See, Ibn Kathîr, *Tafsîr*, II, 219.

In a Prophetic saying we read: "Eat, drink, dress yourself, and give charity without falling into profligacy and arrogance." (Bukhârî, Libâs, 1). This saying indicates the limits the limits that people should observe when they satisfy their needs. In another Prophetic saying, we read: "It would certainly be extravagance to eat everything you desire!" (Ibn Mâja, At'ima, 51).

Greedily devouring everything is what is termed gluttony, and our religion forbids such an action. Again, this saying indicates that having the opportunity to indulge does not justify overindulgence. Indeed when `Umar came across Jâbir , who had a piece of meat in his hand, he asked him, "What is that?"

Jâbir answered: "It is a piece of meat, which I bought because I desired it."

`Umar replied, "Do you buy everything that you desire? Don't you fear that you might be one of those who are described in the verse: '*You spent and exhausted all your good things in the life of the world...*'(Ahkâf 46/20)" (Ibn Hanbal, Zuhd, p.124).

Our Prophet concisely stated the measure one must observe regarding consumption: "No man filled a cup more dangerous than his stomach. Certainly a few bites of food are sufficient to live. But if one has to eat more, let him allow one third of his stomach for food, one third of it for drink, and one third of it for breathing!" (Tirmidhî, Zuhd, 47).

The following event that happened during the Age of Felicity clearly indicates the importance of following the prophetic guidelines concerning the consumption of food and beverage.

Along with many precious gifts, the governor of Alexandria sent our Prophet a physician. Our Prophet said to the physician, "You may go back to your family. We are a community that does not eat unless it gets hungry, and when we eat, we stop before our stomachs are full." (Halabî, *Insân al-ʿUyûn*, III, 299).

These Prophetic statements include the prescription to heal many diseases resulting from the excessive consumption and extravagance commonly observed in our age.

ʿUmar ﷺ gives the following advice in this regard: "Refrain from entirely filling your stomach with food and drink. Otherwise it will be harmful to your body, will encourage the emergence of disease, and will make you lazy about ritual prayer. Follow the middle way regarding the consumption of food and drink! That is more useful to your body, and will also move you away from wastefulness." (Ali al-Muttaqî, *Kanz*, XV, 433/41713).

Thevenôt, a Western traveler, wrote a book of observations made during his travels and published it in Paris in 1665. In that book he recorded how our predecessors, who carried the flag of Islam for so many centuries, organized their lives. He noted their cleanliness and simplicity and their moderation in consumption, and how all these customs resulted in a society of healthy people. He said:

Turks live a healthy life and rarely get sick. Among them, you do not find the diseases related to the kidneys and so many other dangerous diseases that we come across in our homeland. They do not even know their names. I suppose that the reasons why the Turks have such perfect health conditions are that they bathe frequently and are moderate in their consumption of food and beverages. They eat only small amounts of food. And the foods they eat are not mixed, unlike the kind of food commonly eaten among Christians.[45]

45. M. De Thevenot, *Relation d'un Voyage Fait au Levant*, s. 58, Paris, 1665.

A proverb reminds us, "A person should not live to eat, but should eat to live!" The principle describes an important characteristic of believers. The following episode explains this measure of Islamic morality. It is full of lessons.

One day, the Messenger of Allah ﷺ had a guest, who was an unbeliever. The Prophet ﷺ ordered that a sheep should be milked for the guest. They milked the sheep and brought the milk to the guest. The guest drank all the milk that was brought to him. So they brought another pot, and the guest drank all of that. This happened seven times; the guest drank seven pots of milk. The next day the guest embraced Islam. The Messenger of Allah ﷺ again ordered that they should bring milk to the guest. They brought one pot of milk, and the guest finished it. The Prophet ﷺ ordered another pot, and. they brought it, but this time the guest could not drink it all. Upon this the Prophet ﷺ, the pride of the universe, said: "A believer drinks with one intestine, while an unbeliever drinks with seven intestines!" (Muslim, Ashriba', 186).

Allah the Exalted wants us to be moderate in the consumption of food and drink and keep away from the custom that unbelievers follow in this regard. He warns us:

...while those who reject Allah will enjoy (this world) and eat as cattle eat. And the Fire will be their abode. (Muhammad, 47/12)

All behaviors that remove the blessing of the food are included under wastefulness. So if one begins eating without washing one's hands and without remembering Allah, and if one does not thank Allah at the end of the meal, such negligence is considered not only ingratitude, but also profligacy.

In a Prophetic saying we read: "The blessing of the meal is in washing one's hands before and after the meal." (Tirmidhi, At`ima, 39).

"When someone goes to bed without washing the food off his hands, if he experiences harm, let him not blame anybody but himself!" (Abû Dâwûd, At'ima, 53).

Our ancestors were quite careful about washing hands before and after meals. Ricaut, a secretary who worked in the British Consulate in Istanbul in the seventeenth century (and indeed an enemy of the Turks), described the carefulness of our predecessors regarding meal-time hygiene. "Hand-washing is so common a custom among Turks," he remarked, "that they have a proverb that Allah created food so that people might wash their hands!"[46]

Thus observing the rules of hygiene when eating or drinking becomes a means to increase blessing and supports both material and spiritual health and peace. Additionally, if people begin a meal by saying *bismillâh* ("in the name of Allah") and end it with *alhamdulillâh* ("the praise belongs to Allah"), that meal becomes curative, whereas a meal consumed without remembering and thanking Allah produces only negligence and excess weight. Our Prophet ﷺ declared:

If a person says *bismillâh* when entering his house and when beginning his meal, the Devil says to his soldiers, "You can neither spend the night nor find food here." But if a person does not say *bismillâh* when he enters his house, the Devil says to his soldiers, "Here is a place for you to spend the night." And if that person does not say *bismillâh* when he begins to eat, the Devil says to his soldiers, "You have found both a place to stay the night and something to eat." (Muslim, Ashriba', 103)

A'ishah ﷺ related :

46. Ricaut, *Histoire de l'état Présent de l'Empire Ottoman*, s. 285, Paris, 1670.

Once the Messenger of Allah ﷺ sat down to eat with six of his Companions. A Bedouin came; he ate all the food in two bites. Then our Prophet ﷺ said, "If he had said *bismillâh*, the food would have been enough for all of us. Thus when any of you begins eating, let him say *bismillâh*. If he forgets to say it at the beginning, let him say *bismillâh fi awwâlihi wa akhirihi*, "In the name of Allah be its beginning and its end."

When drinking water, the proper manners are to say *bismillâh* and to drink it in three sips; at the end one should say *alhamdulillâh*. Our Prophet ﷺ used to drink water and other beverages by dividing them into three parts. He said, "Don't drink things down all at once, as camels do. Drink in two or three sips. Pronounce *bismillâh* before you drink something; and at the end say *alhamdulillâh*. (Tirmidhî, Ashriba, 13). Our Prophet ﷺ also forbade blowing into a beverage for any reason.

A certain man asked him, "What shall I do if I see that something dirty has fallen into the water jar?"

The Messenger of Allah said, "Pour the fallen thing out!"

Then the man said, "I don't feel that my thirst is quenched when I drink." The Messenger of Allah suggested that he drink the water divided into three parts, and added, "Then take the cup of water away from your mouth!" (Tirmidhî, Ashriba', 15)

Eating alone also decreases the blessing in the food, and is a kind of wastefulness.. Our Prophet ﷺ said that "There is compassion in community, and fire in solitude." He advised us to be together when we eat.

Wahshî b. Harb ﷺ related that some Companions said, "O Messenger of Allah! We eat but we do not feel satisfied."

The Messenger of Allah asked, "Perhaps you have your meals alone?"

They said, "Yes, we do!"

The Messenger of Allah told them, "Have your meals together and say *bismillâh*, so that your food becomes blessed." (Abû Dâwûd, At`ima, 14)

The Prophet ﷺ also warned us, "If one of you drops a bite of food and it gets dirty, let him clean the dirt off and eat his bite. Do not leave it to the Devil." Continuing his warning, he encouraged us to eat all the food on our plates. "You do not know where the blessing of the meal is found," he said. (Muslim, Ashriba', 136).

One feels terribly shaken when one sees the wastefulness dominating our habits of consumption of food and drink, in our daily life and especially during wedding ceremonies and feasts. At such times the amount of waste is immeasurable. We may form a rough idea of our wastefulness by watching our consumption of bread. Although it is difficult to precisely measure the amount of waste involved in other sorts of expenses, we may form some estimate by watching what happens with loaves of bread. The estimated results are frightening.

Preparing ostentatious banquets to show off pride and power, encouraging gluttony with all-you-can-eat meals, strutting about foolishly in expensive designer clothes – all these excessive behaviors will certainly bring regret in the Hereafter, since we shall be questioned on these expenditures according to the divine measure.

Wedding ceremonies and banquets are important means for strengthening community feeling. Unfortunately, when such celebrations are designed egotistically, for purposes of show, they do not function to build community feeling. Instead they push people toward evil sentiments like pride, arrogance, jealousy, and envy, which lead to disappointment. Communities where such celebrations are encouraged fall away from the divine mercy and blessing.

To sum up, the end of a life controlled by extravagance is such a huge disappointment that Allah the Almighty says:

The profligate are the friends of devils. (Isrâ, 17/27)

The Messenger of Allah reminded us that in the Hereafter we shall be required to give an accounting of all the bounties and trusts that we received during our worldly life. He urged us to move away from negligence. "No servant of Allah will be able to leave his place before he provides an explanation of where he spent his life, what he achieved with his knowledge, how he earned his wealth and how spent it, and how he spent the strength of his body." (Tirmidhî, Qiyâmah, 1)

Thus we should never forget that going beyond the divinely set limits with regard to consumption of food and drink is wastefulness. Neglecting the bounty of health and thus losing it is wastefulness. Spending our lifetime in vain is grave wastefulness. Neglecting to protect the material and spiritual trusts in our care, orienting our thoughts and feelings in wrong directions – these are also wastefulness. Especially in the area of education, which is the making of human personality, neglecting to help other human beings to understand that they are the most honored of creatures, and thus losing them, is a most serious wastefulness.

Certainly it is an indispensable task for parents to provide their children education that promotes adoption of the Qur'an and the Prophetic tradition. This education should be such that it prevents the loss of children's spiritual life. Efforts in this direction also show how much we love the Qur'an and the Prophet ﷺ, and abide by them. As the Prophet ﷺ declared, "I have entrusted two things to you: the Book and the Tradition (Sunnah)." (Muwatta', Qadar, 3).

Thus we must make efforts to increase our love for the noble Qur'an. And we must pay close attention to the spiritual and moral formation of our children, since these are usually neglected in the formal life of education.

Indeed the most precious legacy that we may leave to our children is the culture of the noble Qur'an and the Prophetic tradition. We must try hard to lead our children to adopt the Prophetic moral traits, which means the implementation of the Qur'anic guidelines with full acceptance. We should not waste their eternal life in exchange for concerns regarding their temporary life.

In this regard, if we love our children, if we want to protect them from all kinds of danger, and if we want to be together with them in the Hereafter, we must make efforts to be sure that they receive an education that incorporates the tenets of faith. Allah the Almighty states how efforts in this regard become a means of happiness in the Hereafter:

Those who believe and whose seed follow them in faith, We cause their seed to join them (there), and we deprive them of nothing of their (life's) work. Every person is a pledge for that which he has earned. (at-Tûr, 52/21)

Those believers who receive this blessing shall be together with their faithful progeny in the Hereafter. It is an exceptional divine grace bestowed upon them, that they should live in Paradise together with their children. In this way the joy and happiness of parents become perfect. The condition of receiving such a grace is that our children be educated as faithful generations, raised within the atmosphere of the noble Qur'an and the Prophetic tradition.

To fulfill our duty toward our children concerning the life of the Hereafter is a heavy responsibility that we take upon our shoulders. Let us keep far away from the "waste of human resources" that is the gravest of all kinds of profligacy.

⊗

If our most important activities are analyzed in the light of the measures we have now identified as relevant to profligacy, we will see how extensive the application of this concept truly is. Wastefulness categorizes a wide range of behaviors that manifest in a variety of forms in every area of our lives, from too much hatred and too much love to the ostentation in celebrations and banquets.

What we have done so far is to attempt to identify usable standards and to point in the general direction of their implementation by analyzing a few essential issues. But the standards and attitudes we have tried to identify here are not bound to the topics mentioned: they are applicable to all kinds of human actions. Thus we should not forget that it is our responsibility to apply these standards wherever they turn out to be applicable, and so keep away from all kinds of extravagance and miserliness.

May Allah the Almighty keep us away from the extremes of either too little or too much! May He help us to achieve a life of servanthood that pleases Him! May He guide us so that we use all of His bounties according to the great principle of moderation, and may we thank Him for them properly!

Amin…

"There is No Excuse For Violating The Boundary between Lawful and Unlawful Acts"

An Interview Concerning Islamic Sensitivity in The Business World

Unlawful income is like a balloon that suddenly explodes. Some of these balloons blow up in this life, and some of them blow up in the Hereafter. The apparent increase in such income may look very pleasant, but its spiritual reality is thoroughly disappointing. Unlawful income leads to eternal bankruptcy.

In order to estimate the spiritual level of our income, we can examine where we spend it. Just as the proverb says, "Money is like a snake: it goes out the same hole it came in."

"THERE IS NO EXCUSE FOR VIOLATING THE BOUNDARY BETWEEN LAWFUL AND UNLAWFUL ACTS"

An Interview Concerning Islamic Sensitivity in the Business World

Dear Ustadh: These days people debate the relationship between Islam and capitalism, and argue that Muslims are becoming supporters of capitalism. What do you have to say about this issue?

The places where capitalism emerges and develops are places where attitudes such as contentment and trust in Allah grow weaker, and strong cravings for the world, and consequently the attractions of unlawful earnings, grow much stronger. Because of the power of such attractions, Muslims should subject themselves to Sufi education in order control their anxieties and cravings. Control of these can be obtained through consciously cultivating contentment and trusting one's affairs to Allah.

Contentment is the true wealth. It means freedom from the craving for money and possessions, a craving that makes people slaves to property. But if a Muslim does not cleanse his ego and purify his heart, he may find himself miserably enmeshed in capitalistic processes, which recognize no limit but money.

Neither the capitalist nor the socialist system leaves any room for the merits of the heart and the virtues of conscience. One claims that property belongs to society; the other claims that it belongs to individuals. Both are shaped by a mentality that seeks self-interest and exploitation. In both these systems, persons are like cogs of a wheel.

According to Islam, property belongs to Allah. When one holds such a view, there is no room for seeking self-interest and exploitation. Islamic economics begins with solving the problems of human life. Sharing one's possessions and helping others, especially those who are in need, is a stipulation of the religion, a compulsory duty. Allah the Almighty has declared that the poor have a claim on the wealth of the rich.

Those who ask (are in need) and those who are deprived (cannot beg because of their dignity) have a definite share in their (the wealthy's) property. (Zâriyât 51/19)

This principle is a kind of education concerning the use of money, as well as a means of bringing people together. That is, according to the Islamic principle, money is not an object of desire to be accumulated, but a trust that needs spending. If it is spent or used properly, if the shares of the needy and the poor are delivered, then wealth becomes a great opportunity for serving Allah. However, as the pre-condition of realizing these ends, it is quite important to pay attention to where and how the money is earned. Indeed, for everything that may be earned there is a certain way that it should be earned. According to the way the money is earned, the heart of the earner is shaped. Then the way money is spent depends on the shape of the heart, the personality, of the one who spends it. Hence we must be extremely careful about the way we earn our livings.

What kinds of incomes are there?

There seem to be two kinds of incomes. The first is income regularly earned according to the religious rules and principles of conscience, which are based on the observation of divinely set limits. This includes trade, which has its own moral principles.

Lawfulness in any kind of earning is indispensable: there is no justification for a mania of self-interest leading to the deception of others. Even though one's earnings may not accumulate rapidly when they are made lawfully, their spiritual value will always increase. Such wealth always allocates some amount for charity, for supporting good and beautiful things. This brings the individual peace of conscience. Those Muslims who govern their property according to such rules are merciful toward all creatures, and for human beings to display mercy is the only means of drawing divine mercy towards us all. The Messenger of Allah announced, "Be merciful to those who are on earth, so that those who are in the heavens may be merciful to you!" (Tirmidhî, Birr, 16)

The moral history of money influences the feelings of its possessor. In order to estimate the spiritual level of our income, we can examine where we spend it. Just as the proverb says, "Money is like a snake: it goes out the same hole it came in."

What about the other kind?

The second kind of income is that obtained by means of some authority or power. This kind of income is generally unlawful. It is accumulated by doing unjust favors and accepting bribes. In a sense it is cancerous wealth.

Unlawful income is like a balloon that suddenly explodes. Some of these balloons blow up in this life, and some of them blow up in the Hereafter. The apparent increase in such income may look very pleasant, but its spiritual reality is thoroughly disappointing. Unlawful income leads to eternal bankruptcy.

Such wealth can rarely be spent for charity, for supporting good and beautiful things. At most a little bit of it will be an exception....

Unfortunately, nowadays the second kind of income seems attractive to everybody. The capitalist order encourages this kind of wealth. It is quite sad that so many believers seem to take it into their hearts as well. So many people contract the craving for money.

The thing to do before pursuing any form of income is to calculate how you are going to explain it in the Hereafter. When hearts grow insensitive and people cease to care about the Hereafter, they easily turn into savages who do not recognize conscience or law, merciless usurpers of rights. By its exploitation of human anxieties and desires, capitalism pushes people toward savagery. We may find examples around the world to support this. People are abused merely for the sake of money. How can such an attitude combine with human values? It leads to the development and use of bombs that do not discriminate: plants and animals, children and adults, the sick and elderly all become targets. There is no mercy, no tenderness. Can money stained with the blood of the innocent and the poor possibly build or restore humanity? Yet such is the wealth of the merciless capitalism that subjugates humanity to money day after day. It turns money into an idol for worship.

Then what kind of a framework does Islam suggest?

Just as in other affairs, Islam considers servants responsible to Allah with regard to money. This is because Allah the Exalted bestowed everything upon human beings as a trust. In the noble Qur'an we read:

Then, you shall be questioned that day about the profit (you took) (at-Takâthur 102/8).

Thus one should acquire wealth according to the measures of consideration and responsibility. There is no excuse for violating the boundary between lawful and unlawful acts. To say "I am acquiring this wealth in order to be able to do good things in the future," is a bad direction to take: it is merely self-deception. Islam can never approve the principle of "earn as you like, and spend as you like!" So Muslims must undoubtedly reject the basic theory of capitalism: unlimited accumulation and consumption.

Today, in a period when human beings are subjugated to material gains, every Muslim must have higher moral character than ever before. He or she must behave with the fear of Allah, be extremely respectful toward the rights of others, and maintain a sense of personal responsibility.

For example, Muslims must refrain from procuring unjust financing to get through commercial difficulties or economic recessions. We should overcome our financial problems by obtaining help from Islamic financial institutions. Keeping away from paying or receiving interest is a very important issue with regard both to our responsibilities in this life and the state of our life in the Hereafter.

Another issue to which we must pay attention in order to keep ourselves and our property spiritually clean is to refrain from bribes offered for contracts under the guise of gifts or tips. You may change the name of an act, but its nature remains the same. New terms for old unlawful behaviors are a useless attempt to console ourselves about what we do: they are veneers of Hell that prevent us from interrogating our actions. Abdullah ibn ʿAmr 🞋, one of the Companions of the Messenger of Allah, related that the Prophet 🞋

cursed both those who take bribes and those who offer them. (Abû Dâwûd, `Aqdiyyah, 4:3580).

Unfortunately, these days wealth is poisoned by this custom, and many related customs, on all sides. If a Muslim is not as careful, attentive and informed as if he would be if he were walking through a minefield, he cannot protect his wealth from these poisons.

What kind of care, attention, and sensitivity are you advising?

We must shape our commercial lives not according to the exploitation and self-interest of capitalism, but by a determined observance of the boundary between the lawful and the unlawful.

Again, we should protect ourselves from organizing our affairs in the service of an economic system that encourages wastefulness. The increase of extravagance and luxury severely damages society. Credit cards, which cause the increase in spending, are also economic traps: they are means of exploitation. Being in need cannot justify their use. Islam offers a better solution to those who have needs but no money: *qard hasan* (well-managed debt for the sake of Allah). This kind of debt is designed to relieve those who have financial difficulties and help them to recover. It is credit given to the needy without asking for any interest. The kind of debt provided by credit cards, however, leads to the bankruptcy of their users. It is a system in which the winners are those who make you spend, but not those who do the spending.

Advertising lead you to spend so that other people behind the scenes may use you to make money. In this cause they exploit even the poor, without feeling any responsibility. Fascinated by deceptive advertisements, many poor people are victimized by following illegal procedures. For example, an advertisement may put out the message, "A young girl will look great only if she uses such-and-such a product! If you do this and that, you will be very attractive and sought after!" Having seen the advertisement, the poor girl becomes full of desire and anxious to get those things. But since she lacks the money to afford them, she may begin to live immorally and destroy her life...

Thus we must always remember that the greatest wealth is to be content and satisfied with our lot. Allah the Almighty did not command us: "Be rich!" His command is: "Earn your sustenance lawfully, spend it lawfully, and give charity!" If we never forget the needy, we will establish our commercial life on a lawful foundation.

It seems that Muslims who observe religious commandments change their commitment at times.

Unfortunately, today capitalism has destroyed our spiritual world so much that even in companies whose owners have religious sensitivities, it has become natural to carry out business in a manner contrary to Islamic ethics and ideals. There are so many people who perform their daily prayers regularly and have made the Pilgrimage to Mecca, yet argue, "I must earn more so that I can give more charity!" But this argument cannot be justified. That is, in many cases you see the mixture of the lawful and the unlawful. Take for example advertising claims made without any moral concern, or female secretaries who are hired specifically to attract customers. These are clearly unacceptable things. When we emphasize the wealth of the world more than the revenue of the Hereafter, our selfishness will always excuse itself by saying, "That's just how things are!" The lower soul does not care about the prohibited aspects of the business in question. Unfortunately, this is not real wealth. It is a mine of bankruptcy that will explode in the Hereafter.

Thus, in commercial life, each and every issue must be carefully studied. We must be careful of whom we employ, and should never violate Islamic rules for any reason whatsoever. We should not force women to do men's work, or force men do women's work: people should never be compelled to do anything contrary to their nature. Our ultimate guidelines must be Islamic ethics and principles that set the highest standards. In the light of the divine warnings about our conduct of affairs, we must be careful of our duties as servants and the rights of other people over us.

Before he died, our Prophet ﷺ commanded, "Be careful of the ritual prayer, and be fearful of Allah concerning the rights of those who are under your rule!" (Abû Dâwûd, Adab, 123-124/5156; Ibn Mâja, Wasâyâ, 1). He had been careful throughout his life about the rights of all creatures, yet just before his death our Prophet ﷺ did something that dramatically underlined the importance of the rights of other people. Though he was very weak, he went to the mosque and said to his Companions, "O my companions, if I have taken the wealth of any of you without being aware of it, here is my property: let him come out and take his right!. And if I have struck any of you, here is my back: let him come forward and strike!..." (See Ahmad, III, 400).

Upon hearing these words, the Companions began to weep.

These words show us the importance of the rights of other people. By them, the Prophet ﷺ provided a model to his community – a model that can be imitated by his community until the Last Day. It is our duty to behave ourselves according to the guidelines provided by this example.

Abuse of the rights of other people is the kind of violent ignorance and injustice that will remain until the Day of Judgment, and that will always lead those responsible for it to eternal destruction.

Today, capitalism does not respect the rights of others. It oppresses further those who are oppressed already. Capitalists consider everything permissible. But for Muslims, there are things that must be forbidden.

In sum, today we need a deep self-criticism, a shaking up that will bring us to consciousness! For at present, capital has precedence over persons. However, persons must take precedence over capital.

How can we achieve this, since money is the essence of capitalism and everything revolves around it?

In order to achieve this we must rule money but not be ruled by it. And this, in turn, can be achieved by following the commands of the Ruler of rulers.

Look around you. There are many people with abundant material opportunities, but they are not peaceful. Some fall into insanity. Compared to earlier times, the level of wealth and welfare has increased greatly – but cases of depression and madness have also increased. Family life has been damaged. Cases of divorce have increased. Children experience terrible situations. A generation that is deprived of a peaceful family environment looks for its happiness in the streets. And it is simply left to the mercy of the streets. The selfish capitalist system, which does not recognize the distinction between lawful and unlawful, has not brought peace to our society.

Nurettin Topçu, with whom I took classes during my Imam-Hatip high school education, used to ask us, "Who is happier, people today, or people who lived in the past?" Then he would answer the question in detail, explaining how the people of the past were happy and how contemporary people lack peace and mercy.

Dear Ustadh, being wealthy seems to be a difficult trial.

Depending on conditions, both being wealthy and being poor can be difficult trials. Neither was ever easier than the other. Thus you should not take my words to mean that in order to be peaceful, one must be poor! My emphasis on our responsibilities and the importance of observing the divine limits should not result in your misunderstanding that poverty should be encouraged. One should know that Islam never prohibits people from getting rich. To the contrary, we read the command "*Give charity!*" more than two hundred times in the noble Qur'an. This may be taken as advice that people acquire enough wealth to be able to give charity. The point we would like to make is that one should not push too far the limits of the divine division of property, which are the limits of fate. One should not consider all means to be lawful in order to get wealthy. Yet it is necessary to earn the degree of lawful sustenance allotted to us by Allah, and to acquire the virtue of being able to give charity.

In fact, we need merciful people with lawful earnings who accumulate enough wealth to support those who are poor and needy. They were needed in the past, and they are needed today.

The point is that we should not lose peace of heart for the sake of material welfare. We should not destroy the peace of heart that results from the beauties of Islam. We should be people of love, and never forget that the true and endless wealth is found in the life of the heart.

Might we take as an example Abû Hanîfah, who engaged in commerce and who was also a great Muslim scholar?

Yes, certainly. Abû Hanîfah (founder of the Hanafi school of religious jurisprudence, which is followed by the vast majority of Turks) is an exemplary figure in regard to good practice, as well as in regard to scholarship. His morally praiseworthy, indeed ideal,

behavior in his commercial transactions displays the noble properties one would look for in a major Muslim personality. We might
say that we need a campaign to uphold moral values like those of
Abû Hanîfah in today's society, in which the feeling of solidarity
has weakened, social peace and tranquility are lost, and hatred and
animosity have become common. Here is one of the many stories
about him.

Abû Hanîfah was a wealthy person who earned his livelihood
through commercial activities. Since he was occupied with scholarship, studying and teaching, he employed agents to carry out the
commercial activities on his behalf. Abû Hanîfah would monitor
whether the agents' activities were compatible with religious rules.
He was extremely careful in this regard. Once he sent his business
partner Hafs ibn `Abdurrahman to sell cloth. He said to him, "O
Hafs! This package of cloth has this and that deficiency. So let the
customers know of its defects, and sell the package at such-and-
such a discount."

Hafs sold that package of cloth at the price identified by Abû
Hanîfah. However, he forgot to tell the purchaser about the cloth's
defects. When Abû Hanîfah learned of the situation, he asked Hafs
ibn `Abdurrahman, "Do you know the customer who bought that
cloth?" Hafs said that he did not..

Hearing this, Imam Abû Hanîfah gave everything he had
earned on the transaction to charity. He feared that the money
received for goods with undisclosed faults would spoil the lawfulness of his earning. This kind of behavior, which resulted from his
fear of Allah, brought divine blessing to the material as well as to the
spiritual commerce of Abû Hanîfah.

In order to understand whether a person is virtuous, sincere
and honest, we must consider not the acts of worship he performs,

but the spiritual state in which he performs his actions. That is, we must consider whether his behavior is compatible with Islamic morality and whether his income is acquired in lawful ways. In this regard, when somebody praised a certain person to ʿUmar 🕮, he asked three things: "Have you ever lived in the same neighborhood with that person? Have you ever traveled together with him? Have you ever had commercial dealings with him?" The praiser said "no" to all these things. ʿUmar said, "Then don't praise him, because you do not know him properly."

In the same vein, Sufyân as-Sarwî 🕮 said, "The degree of one's spiritual state corresponds to the degree that one's bread is lawfully earned." One day, somebody asked him, "O master! Could you please tell us the value of performing the ritual prayer in the first line at the mosque?" Instead, he started talking about the importance of lawful earning. Then he said, "O my brother! First pay attention to how you obtain your food! If your earning is lawful, then go and pray in whichever line you want. You will find no difficulty in this regard."

My deceased father Musa Efendi 🕮 used to tell the following story to indicate how very important and blessed it is for people to earn their livelihood in lawful ways, and to avoid contaminating their earnings with unlawful ingredients.

We had a non-Muslim neighbor. Later on he accepted Islam. One day I asked him why he had done so. He told me: "I became Muslim thanks to the noble moral principles Rebî Molla practiced in his business.. He and I had neighboring lands. Rebî Molla used to earn his livelihood by selling milk. One evening he came to our house and said, "Here you are, this bucket of milk is yours!"

I was surprised. I said, "How can this be? I didn't ask you for milk!"

He was a delicate and sensitive person. He said, "I saw that one of my animals was grazing in your garden. I could not tell when it had entered your garden, or how far it had gone. That is why this bucket of milk is yours. Until the end of its digestive cycle, I will be bringing you its milk."

I exclaimed, "There's no problem, neighbor! It's only grass and plants. I don't claim any rights over you!"

But Molla Rebî said, "No, no, I cannot accept that. This milk is your right!" And he brought us the milk of that animal until its digestive cycle was over.

The behavior of that virtuous man touched me, and helped remove the veils from my eyes. Thus the sun of divine guidance rose. I said to myself: "The religion of a man with such a noble character must certainly be the best of religions. Who could doubt the truth of a religion when its followers are so refined, so appreciative of the rights of others, so perfect and sincere?" So I said the words of testimony and became a Muslim myself."

These models seem too lofty to be realized in our money-centered world. But of course there are many good examples! Finally, could you give us some direct advice?

These wise stories show us clearly how much care we should take in the matter of lawful and unlawful earning. Indeed, lawful earning is an essential part of *taqwa*, mindfulness of Allah.. This is why we read in a saying the Prophet ﷺ, "The honest and reliable laborer shall be found together with the Messengers of Allah, the people of sincerity, and the martyrs." (Tirmidhî, Buyû', 4). This is because a working person who has a sensitive heart becomes an agent bringing peace and blessing to all who meet him. He thus earns happiness both in this world and in the Hereafter. However, for those who are defeated by the craving for this world, the situation is different. Although they may seem to have magnificent worldly lives, they are destitute and deprived with regard to the endless life of the Hereafter.

The Prophet ﷺ did not count as members of his community those who were greedy in commerce and deceived others. He excluded them. We have the following report.

One day the Prophet ﷺ visited a merchant in the marketplace. He plunged his hand into the man's pile of wheat, and felt that it was wet. He asked, "What is this?"

The man answered: "Rain made it wet, O Messenger of Allah!"

The Prophet ﷺ said: "Could not you leave the wet part on the surface, so that your customers would see it? Those who deceive us, do not belong to us." (Muslim, Imân, 164).

Again the Messenger of Allah said: "Every community has a trial. The trial of my community is wealth." (Ahmad ibn Hanbal, IV, 160)

And: "There will come a time when people will not care whether they earn their property in lawful ways or unlawful ones." (Bukhârî, Buyû', 7, 23).

And: "I fear that after I leave you, you will be presented with the flowers (goods) and ornaments of the world. And you may fall in love with them!" (Bukhârî, Jihâd, 37; Muslim Zakâh, 121-123).

And once, addressing his Companions, the Prophet ﷺ declared, "I do not fear poverty for you. But I fear that the world will be spread before you, as it was spread before earlier generations. And I fear that just as earlier generations did, you will compete for it. And

I fear that just as the world destroyed earlier generations, so it will destroy you." (Bukhârî, Riqâq 7, Jizya 1; Muslim, Zuhd, 6).

This saying seems to summarize contemporary conditions. People who manifest the negligence indicated in the sayings of the Prophet ﷺ may find it very difficult to leave unlawful acts. And if their hearts cannot leave the unlawful, it will be a great challenge, and constitute an act of worship, if they attempt to hold on to the lawful.

Today, Muslims must try hard to protect ourselves from the evils of capitalism. Beware of making money an object of anxiety and desire! Instead, let us assume the characteristics suitable to virtuous believers. Under all conditions, let us be mindful of Allah, seek the divine acceptance, act compassionately in society, absorb the principles of Islamic ethics, respect the rights of others, and observe the limits of lawful and unlawful things.

Remember that, given contemporary conditions, every just and merciful heart must feel the pain of the poor, the weak, and the grieving. But those who truly deserve to be pitied are

• conscienceless oppressors, even more than the helpless they oppress;

• slaves to their egos, despite their luxurious lives;

• greedy-hearted exploiters, even more than the needy they exploit.

These truly miserable people require more mercy than others. Our sense of pity and mercy is a way to save them from the terrible situations into which they have fallen, and may help them to find guidance toward the path of truth.

Our Prophet ﷺ said: "O my Allah! I take refuge in you from useless knowledge, from the insensitive heart, from the unsatisfied stomach, and from the unacceptable prayer." (Muslim, Dhikr, 73).

And: "Hurry up, before you fall either into the poverty that makes people forget, or into the wealth that leads people astray!" (See, Tirmidhî, Zuhd, 3/2306)

So let us always remember what the Prophet ﷺ stated here: that the poverty that makes people forget Allah, and the wealth that leads them astray from Him, may be considered equal.

May Allah the Almighty cause all of us to live surrounded by divine beauties! May He keep us away from all unlawful or suspect things!.

Amîn...